Hunger for the Word

Lectionary Reflections on Food and Justice

Year A

Edited by

Larry Hollar

1106

LITURGICAL PRESS

Collegeville, Minnesota

www.litpress.org

1   2   3   4   5   6   7   8   9

Library of Congress Cataloging-in-Publication Data

Hunger for the Word: lectionary reflections on food and justice / edited by Larry Hollar.
    p. cm.
  Includes bibliographical references and index.
    ISBN 0-8146-2920-2 (Year A : pbk. : alk. paper) — ISBN 0-8146-3008-1 (Year B : pbk. : alk. paper) — ISBN 0-8146-3009-X (Year C : pbk. : alk. paper)
  1. Bible—Meditations. 2. Food—Religious aspects—Christianity—Meditations. 3. Hunger—Religious aspects—Christianity—Meditations. I. Hollar, Larry, 1948–

BS680.F6H86 2004
261.8'326—dc22

                                                            2003021080

Dedicated to

the skilled, committed, and Spirit-filled

Bread for the World members

and all the people of faith

in our nation and world

who struggle to end the scandal of hunger

in God's beloved world

Contents

Acknowledgments

This book would not exist without the generous support of:

- Bread for the World and Bread for the World Institute, which granted me a four-month sabbatical to edit the initial drafts of the text and additional time and resources to prepare the succeeding drafts and final version;

- The Churches' Center for Theology and Public Policy at Wesley Theological Seminary in Washington, D.C., which graciously offered me a position as Visiting Scholar and abundant resources and warm support during my sabbatical;

- The fourteen writers of this book, who were amazingly prompt in providing manuscripts and responding to comments and were profoundly dedicated to making this a valuable resource for the faith-based, anti-hunger advocacy movement;

- Bread for the World members Anne Iott and Helen Siegl, whose artwork enlivens the cover and pages of this book;

- Kathy Pomroy, Jim McDonald, Barbara Green, John Crossin, and numerous Bread for the World activists, who provided the initial encouragement to undertake the project and valuable insights that shaped both the content of the book and choices about writing, editing, and publication;

- Colleagues of the faculty, staff, and student body at Wesley Seminary, who offered helpful comments on the book's progress and ideas that supported both my spiritual and analytical processes during my sabbatical;

- Ken South and my Bread for the World Organizing Department and other colleagues, who suggested potential writers for the book, picked up the slack when the book responsibilities intruded on my organizing duties at Bread, and offered daily encouragement to see the task to completion;

- The editorial staff at the Liturgical Press, who embraced the idea of this book as a way to link justice and liturgy in intimate and compelling ways and who brought this work to life, especially my very able copy editor, John Schneider, and art editor, Ann Blattner;

- My wife Karen Cassedy, without whose support and encouragement this work would never have begun and whose company I enjoyed on our joint commute to Wesley Seminary, even as I plotted to inflict on her countless additional hours of solitude while I finished the editing task.

Introduction

This book and the two other volumes that are part of the *Hunger for the Word* series are for people who love to explore and tussle with the Bible, regularly and respectfully. It is for those who are open to being changed by a consistent, yearning Word that testifies to God's deep love and special care for the world's hungry people. It is for those who seek justice and who value liturgy as the way we praise the God who embodies justice. Reading these pages may be risky business for you, but it's also a hope-filled and "Spirited" venture.

When we look carefully at the Bible, it is clear that the blessing of food and the need to speak out for vulnerable people who lack food are not some marginal afterthoughts or occasional footnotes in the Word. These issues are integral to the identity of those who worship the God of Israel and who follow Jesus Christ. In raising up leaders in the midst of famine in Egypt, in offering manna to the vulnerable Hebrew people in the wilderness, in blessing the Sabbath gleanings of hungry disciples, in feeding multitudes on a remote hillside—God's gracious provision of food never seems far from the heart of the scriptural story. Just as Scripture describes how seemingly barren women produce abundant new life, so too does food and its availability help to define God's graciousness and underscore human dependence on God for what sustains life itself.

Many books written in the past decades have highlighted the wealth of biblical references to matters of hunger, poverty, and justice, and the need for people of faith to respond and speak out about them.[1] Likewise, other authors have explored the richness of the cycle of

1. These include Ronald J. Sider, ed., *Cry Justice!: The Bible on Hunger and Poverty* (Downers Grove, Ill.: InterVarsity Press, 1980), 2nd edition: *For They Shall Be Fed: Scripture Readings and Prayers for a Just World* (Dallas: Word, 1997); Arthur Simon, *Christian Faith and Public Policy: No Grounds for Divorce* (Grand Rapids, Mich.: William B. Eerdmans Publishing Company, 1987) 14–29; *Economic Justice for All: Pastoral Letter on Catholic Social Teaching and the U.S. Economy* (Washington, D.C.: National Conference of Catholic Bishops, 1986) 16–32.

biblical Lectionary readings, noting the themes of biblical justice that emerge throughout the church's liturgical year.[2]

It may be wise to stop for a moment for readers who may be unfamiliar with the word "Lectionary" that appears in the subtitle of this volume and that we begin to use here. A Lectionary is an orderly sequence of selected biblical passages which, when read day by day or week by week for two or three years, are intended to give readers a relatively comprehensive sense of the main themes in both testaments of the Christian Scripture. Daily or weekly lectionaries usually include passages from four parts of the Bible: one passage from the Old Testament (the Hebrew Scriptures), another from the psalms, another from one of the four Gospels, and another from the other New Testament texts (Epistles, Acts, Revelation). When we use the word "Lectionary" in this volume, we mean one of the weekly, three-year cycles of readings that many faith traditions—Roman Catholic, Episcopalian, Lutheran, and various Protestant traditions—use today as a tool for preaching, study, and devotions. Not every parish or congregation in these traditions regularly uses the Lectionary, and some faith groups seek more freedom and openness to the Spirit for sermons and Bible study than the Lectionary's prescribed readings offer. But an increasing number of churches are finding the Lectionary helpful, just as more churches are mindful of the structure and order of the liturgical year as a resource for the church's life.

As the various lectionaries now in use developed, compilers adopted somewhat different approaches to exploring the Bible, so the sequence of readings is not always uniform from one Lectionary to another. In more recent times, efforts have been made to bring the various lectionaries into a greater degree of harmony.[3] As described below, *Hunger for the Word* engages the readings in two widely used lec-

---

2. Dieter Hessel, ed., *Social Themes of the Christian Year: A Commentary on the Lectionary* (Philadelphia: Geneva Press, 1983); *Share Your Bread: World Hunger and Worship. A Lectionary-based Planning Guide* (Chicago: Evangelical Lutheran Church in America, 2000); Walter Burghardt, S.J., *Let Justice Roll Down Like Waters: Biblical Justice Homilies Throughout the Year* (New York/Mahwah, N.J.: Paulist Press, 1998). Burghardt and Fr. Raymond Kemp have done significant work to revitalize social justice preaching in the Church, especially in Catholic settings, through the Preaching the Just Word program sponsored by the Woodstock Theological Center, www.georgetown.edu/centers/woodstock/pjw.htm.

3. Useful books that describe the processes leading to the various lectionaries and the challenges faced in compiling them include Horace T. Allen, Jr., and Joseph P. Russell,

tionaries: the Revised Common Lectionary (RCL), a version in use primarily in Protestant churches, and the 1998 Roman Catholic Lectionary for Mass (LM). The decision to use both sources in this book (although with a primary focus on the Revised Common Lectionary) reflects the broadly ecumenical nature of the Bread for the World movement and the wide range of faith groups that are working together to end hunger.

As lectionaries have come into wider use in worship and Bible study in recent years, a gratifying number of associated resources are now available. Some offer valuable commentary on the assigned Lectionary passages, while others suggest hymns, anthems, solos, and other musical and artistic ideas, as well as liturgical aids such as litanies and prayers. Among these resources are weekly reflections offered in magazines such as *The Christian Century* and *Sojourners*, and compiled volumes that challenge Christians to take seriously the call to discipleship by examining the sweep of the Lectionary cycle of readings from a justice perspective.[4]

Yet none of these resources attempts to do exactly what *Hunger for the Word* offers. Let me tell you some essential background and a bit about how this work came about to explain what this three-volume series of books does and why.

Bread for the World (BFW) is a nationwide Christian advocacy movement that seeks justice for the world's hungry people by lobbying our nation's decision makers. Its life is grounded in 50,000 members across the country, who are, for the most part, associated with worshiping Christian communities—in thousands of local churches, on hundreds of college and seminary campuses, and in countless justice groups. These people are not simply "donors" to a cause; they are also activists, writing letters and making phone calls to their members of Congress and meeting with their elected leaders face to face, to urge more effective and compassionate national policies affecting hunger in

---

On Common Ground: The Story of the Revised Common Lectionary (Norwich, Eng.: Canterbury Press, 1998), and Fritz West, *Scripture and Memory: The Ecumenical Hermeneutic of the Three-Year Lectionaries* (Collegeville, Minn.: The Liturgical Press, 1997).

4. Excellent resources are *Living the Word: Reflections on the Revised Common Lectionary, Cycles A, B, and C* (Washington, D.C.: Sojourners, 1996), and Rev. Noelle Damico's provocative and creative devotions, prayers, and children's reflections in the Lectionary-based resources for Micah 6 congregations that emphasize justice, service, and spiritual growth, available at http://www.pcusa.org/pcusa/wmd/hunger/micah6/.

the United States and overseas. They organize letter-writing events, called "Offerings of Letters," in their churches, on their campuses, and in various groups, inviting others to speak out to Congress and the President. They also come together in ecumenical local groups and telephone-tree networks to organize events and prepare concerted and rapid response to action in Washington.

BFW members study the issues and act on what they learn. For these dedicated activists, lobbying Congress and the Administration in Washington is not just political work—it is part of what they feel called to do and be as Christians. Advocacy on hunger is an essential facet of their lives of faith, like breathing out and breathing in.[5]

As they pray and study the Bible, Bread for the World members look to Scripture for insights into the importance of food in God's economy and for challenge and encouragement in responding to the outrageously frequent times when God's children are left without adequate food. From Scripture they learn that God's people are constantly urged to respond in compassion with direct and immediate hunger relief—charity—and also with a commitment to justice that addresses the long-term, structural causes of hunger—advocacy. Both responses are needed if God's vision of bountiful food for all people is to be realized. Bread for the World's role is to foster advocacy, working to change national policies on hunger.

Over the three decades of its life, Bread for the World has published biblical resources that explain the basic call to Christian advocacy and support specific legislative campaigns. But it's clear that BFW members and other people of faith concerned about hunger want even more biblical grounding for their advocacy work. Pastors and lay preachers in particular ask for more help as they consider how to speak in sermons about hunger and justice, how to make hunger understandable to the church's children during worship, and how to incorporate appropriate and compelling music about these themes. When God's people hear from the pulpit about God's unwavering concern for hungry and marginalized people, they realize that speaking out for justice is at the core of Christian faith. In similar ways, those who use the Lectionary for Bible study ask for provocative reflections that enable dialogue about God's deep concern for those who lack daily bread.

---

5. David Beckmann and Arthur Simon, *Grace at the Table: Ending Hunger in God's World* (New York/Mahwah, N.J.: Paulist Press, 1999) 14.

From these hungers—homiletic and reflective—comes this book. It is not a parochial book meant just for Bread for the World members; rather, it is a resource that anyone who values thoughtful alternative and focused voices can pick up and use each week during those yeasty moments of preparing a sermon or Bible study, or while meditating on Scripture.

Forty-six writers with creative skills and varied perspectives—pastors, scholars, and biblically grounded lay members of Bread for the World from across the United States—are contributors to the three volumes of *Hunger for the Word,* published over a period of several years and covering each of the three cycles (A, B, C) of the Lectionary. These writers are drawn from eighteen different faith traditions and from a wide range of ages, experiences, ministries, and passions. What they have written seeks to provide a unique week-by-week perspective on the Lectionary passages. In inviting writers to join this enterprise, I told them this:

> The focus of these reflections should be on the way the passages for that day offer us insights into God's call to respond to those who are hungry and poor, and the general call for God's people to seek justice for people who are marginalized and vulnerable. Since Bread for the World's particular concern is on hunger advocacy (that is, speaking out to our nation's leaders about hunger in the U.S. and in other nations), you are especially invited to reflect on how the passages may address that concern. Since many other available lectionary resources offer commentary on the meaning of the words in the original languages and on the cultural settings of the passages, you do not need to replicate that information. Your task is to creatively experience the passages from the standpoint of one concerned about hunger and justice in our world and offer insights, stories, images, and provocative questions that preachers, study leaders, and others would find useful in wrestling with the passages. I encourage you to write in a way that is stimulative and evocative rather than scholarly and definitive. Your challenge is to constantly have on the lenses of one who, by your commitment to Bread for the World, can see clearly to ask the question, "How is God speaking to me in these passages in a way that shapes my concern and stimulates my speaking out with and for people who are hungry and poor in God's world?"

Each writer was assigned a period ranging from one to eight Sundays or feast days and was asked to reflect on the passages prescribed for those days in the Revised Common Lectionary and, where different, the Roman Catholic Lectionary for Mass. Their ideas both represent and respect the broad ecumenical nature of the Bread for the World movement and the wider community of those seeking justice in our world.

Clearly, the readings for some weeks in the Lectionary offer fewer or less compelling examples of connections with the call to justice for poor and hungry people than those of other weeks. But writers were encouraged to offer what insights they could, consistent with the demand never to twist Scripture's word to fit our own agendas.

As an optional part of their assignment, writers were invited to offer insights into possible approaches for children's sermons or other liturgical times spent with children. Those can be moments when we share the seeds of justice concerns with our receptive young ones. But it's often very hard to put together creative and grounded messages for children. Perhaps these children's time ideas will make that process easier. Writers also were invited, but not required, to provide examples of appropriate hymns and other musical or artistic resources that could be used in worship or Bible study. (See "A Word about Children's Time Reflections and Musical Suggestions" below, pp. xix–xx, for more information on these resources).

With this as background, the following pages offer a life-giving and affirming sense of Scripture's grounding in the struggle for fairness, justice, and love for God's hungry people. As you read these pages, remember that none of us can live without our daily bread. Food is integral to our daily existence. As we pray, in somewhat different ways, the Lord's Prayer/Our Father together each Sunday, we affirm our reliance on God for that sustenance. Thus God's word given to us each week is always about bread. May that word be opened in fresh and nourishing ways to you as you read this book.

Writers for this book present their own personal reflections on the texts. Their ideas do not necessarily reflect the views of Bread for the World or any faith group or organization with which these writers are affiliated.

Should you want to offer your own justice-oriented insights and reflections on these Scripture passages or comment on the contents of this book, please write to Lectionary Feedback, Bread for the World, 50 F Street, NW, Suite 500, Washington, D.C. 20001, or by email at lectionary@bread.org.

LARRY HOLLAR

A Word about Children's Time Reflections
and Musical Suggestions

Each writer for this book was invited, though not required, to provide three parts of the weekly presentation: the reflection on the Lectionary passages, the children's time piece, and the musical suggestions. All writers prepared the reflection on the passages, and their names are indicated in the byline in the text. Some writers also prepared the other two parts, while others decided not to.

If there are no initials in brackets at the beginning of the children's time piece or the musical suggestions, that means the writer of the Lectionary reflection also prepared those parts. The bracketed initials indicate that another writer is solely responsible for those parts of the weekly presentation. The bracketed initials you may find in the children's time pieces and in the musical suggestions are: [DDW] Donald DiXon Williams; [LH] Larry Hollar; [MM] Marc Miller.

The musical suggestions for each week point to hymns and other sacred music that highlight themes in the passages and the Lectionary reflections for that day. These suggestions may be helpful in preparing liturgies on these themes. In listing sources for these musical ideas, the intent is to provide one source in a readily available musical resource—a hymnal or songbook from the faith traditions of Bread for the World members—rather than list all the places the hymn can be found. You may find the same hymn in a hymnal or songbook you use regularly. Often the musical ideas are songs which have a distinctly social justice orientation and which lean toward more contemporary settings and words. This reflects the fact that many current Lectionary resources provide lists of traditional hymns related to the week's passages. Our goal is to suggest additional quality musical settings that are both challenging in their poetry and singable for choirs and congregations.

Each musical suggestion lists the title of the hymn or song, one hymnal or songbook where it is found, and the page number in that source. The initials used to identify these sources are:

Musical Sources

AAH   *African-American Heritage Hymnal* (Chicago: GIA Publications, 2001)

BH   *The Baptist Hymnal* (Nashville: Convention Press, 1991)

BP   *Banquet of Praise* (Washington, D.C.: Bread for the World, 1990)

CCE   *Cokesbury Chorus Book, Expanded Edition* (Nashville: Abingdon Press, 1999)

CH   *Chalice Hymnal* (St. Louis: Chalice Press, 1995)

EH   *The Hymnal 1982* according to the use of the Episcopal Church (New York: The Church Hymnal Corporation, 1985)

FWS   *The Faith We Sing* (Nashville: Abingdon Press, 2000)

GC   *Gather Comprehensive* (Chicago: GIA Publications, 1994)

LBW   *Lutheran Book of Worship* (Minneapolis: Augsburg Publishing House and Philadelphia: Board of Publication, Lutheran Church in America, 1978)

MBW   *Moravian Book of Worship* (Bethlehem, Penn.: Interprovincial Board of Publications and Communications, 1995)

NB   *The New National Baptist Hymnal* (Nashville: The National Baptist Publishing Board, 1977)

NCH   *The New Century Hymnal* (Cleveland: The Pilgrim Press, 1995)

NHL   *New Hymns for the Lectionary To Glorify the Maker's Name,* music by Carol Doran, words by Thomas H. Troeger (New York: Oxford University Press, 1986)

PH   *The Presbyterian Hymnal* (Louisville: Westminster/John Knox Press, 1990)

PSH   *Psalter Hymnal* (Grand Rapids, Mich.: CRC Publications, 1987, 1988)

RSH   *Renew! Songs and Hymns for Blended Worship* (Carol Stream, Ill.: Hope Publishing Company, 1995)

SF   Jane Parker Huber, *A Singing Faith* (Philadelphia: The Westminster Press, 1987)

SZ   *Songs of Zion* (Nashville: Abingdon Press, 1981)

UMH   *The United Methodist Hymnal* (Nashville: The United Methodist Publishing House, 1989)

WC   *The Worshiping Church: A Hymnal* (Carol Stream, Ill.: Hope Publishing Company, 1990)

WOV   *With One Voice—A Lutheran Resource for Worship* (Minneapolis: Augsburg Fortress, 1995)

Al Krass

First Sunday of Advent

RCL: Isaiah 2:1-5; Psalm 122; Romans 13:11-14; Matthew 24:36-44

LM: Isaiah 2:1-5; Psalm 122:1-2, 3-4, 4-5, 6-7, 8-9; Romans 13:11-14; Matthew 24:37-44

As we begin the Advent season, churches that use liturgical colors can choose purple to denote a penitential period or select blue, which some associate with hope. Either way, there is plenty of related material in our Scripture readings for this and later weeks.

Isaiah's prophetic oracle (vv. 2-4), followed by an exhortation in verse 5, lifts up the hope of all nations for peace and justice, and promises that this shall come to pass. Isaiah uses mythical language—just imagine this in an animated video!—of Mount Zion being raised higher than Sinai or Hermon. Then, under Zion's attractive power, "all the nations shall stream to it."

People come and beckon others to go up to the temple on top of Mount Zion and put themselves in a classroom. There they can learn God's ways so that they might "walk in his paths." They're not just going to talk the talk. They're going to walk the walk. Isaiah then

1

comments that it's out of Zion, out of Jerusalem, that the law—the expression of God's will—will be disseminated to the nations. (We could get into a lot of theological nitpicking here. Don't.) God gives Isaiah the oracle to show him, and through him the people, the goal of all God's activity.

That's revealed, again poetically, in verse 4. Say these words aloud in your study! Recognize that they're among humanity's most treasured hopes. I saw them at the United Nations in New York and at the Peace Palace in The Hague. They have been made into statues and paintings, even under atheistic regimes. The Lord "shall judge between the nations" and bring in a time of equity and justice. Weapons shall be transformed into implements of peace, which will add to the nations' food supply—lots of new plowshares and pruning hooks! These are the "peace dividend" that comes when the obscene sums the nations spend on war-preparedness and war-making are freed up to meet human needs.

This will happen as God's people walk in the might of the Lord. That's what Paul is telling the people in Romans 13: God's hope is close to fulfillment. A "new day" is about to come—the day of salvation. The old ways—the "night"—are "far gone." All this is impelled by God's action, at the time God decides. But, as in Isaiah 2:5, God's work impels the believing community to respond: "Let us then lay aside the works of darkness and put on the armor of light" (Rom 13:12).

Paul lists the behaviors the Roman Christians have to quit doing—individual sins of wild living and bad interpersonal relations. The preacher today must listen to what God is revealing as the besetting sins of our own nights, behaviors that today's people, and particularly we in the United States, must put away. Here are some: materialism, greed and avarice; consumerism gone haywire; the failure of those who have enough to share with those who have not; the insistence of people in our nation of their right to have cheap Middle East oil, to ruin the environment by driving SUVs all over the place, to refuse to use mass transportation or engage in conservation; our nation's unwillingness to develop and use renewable energy; and the U.S.'s giving a smaller percentage of its gross national product to foreign aid than any other major industrial nation. Those are the works of night, the works of the "flesh" and "its desires." None of those behaviors has any place in the daytime. We are to take them off, like old clothes, and put on the new clothes of Jesus Christ (is there a baptismal reference here?)

Now your hearers may not yet be ready to take all this seriously. Here's where the Gospel reading comes in. The people in Noah's day didn't take the imminence of judgment seriously. They kept on living in the same old ways. Again, with God's judgment imminent, believers still are likely to procrastinate, to pay no attention, to fall asleep at the switch. Jesus' words to them and to us are: It's precisely when you least expect it that the judgment is going to come, the final division. It makes no sense, therefore, to wait until you see the events of judgment happening, thinking you'll change your ways then. Start to "watch" now. Change!

Children's Time [LH]

Have the children close their eyes and imagine darkness, then open their eyes to see more light. Tell them that during the Advent season we often imagine ourselves to be in a time of darkness, waiting for the light to arrive as Jesus comes among us. Remind them that even in darkness God is with us. Things that we do in the dark aren't hidden from God. We are deeply loved by God when we are scared and when we are hopeful, in the dark and in the light.

Musical Suggestions

City of God—GC 678

Siyahamb' (We Are Marching in the Light of God)—NCH 526

Al Krass

Second Sunday of Advent

RCL: Isaiah 11:1-10; Psalm 72:1-7, 18-19; Romans 15:4-13; Matthew 3:1-12

LM: Isaiah 11:1-10; Psalm 72:1-2, 7-8, 12-13, 17; Romans 15:4-9; Matthew 3:1-12

Recommendation: Don't harmonize these passages too easily, because they have substantial differences. Paul affirms that the Old Testament text "was written for our instruction, so that by steadfastness and by the encouragement of the scriptures we might have hope" (Rom 15:4). Yet we've got to wrestle with the word—as he did!—before God's word to us today becomes clear.

Isaiah foretells a messianic ruler for Israel who will inaugurate a time of universal harmony. Psalm 72 is a praise-poem, filled with poetic hyperbole, addressed to the then reigning king. John, on the other hand, announces the coming of a fearsome, mighty judge. Only Paul describes an eternal Messiah who inspires hope, joy, and peace.

In both Psalm 72 and Isaiah 11, the ruler is partial to people who are poor. "[W]ith righteousness he shall judge the poor," Isaiah says. It becomes clear in the parallel that this means he will judge *on behalf of* the poor: "and decide with equity *for* the meek of the earth." The psalmist prays that God give the king God's justice so that he may "judge your people with righteousness, and your poor with justice"! (You may want to add verses 12-14, since they bring this point out with crystal clarity.)

When activists call for Third World debt relief, they are often met with the indignant response: "We need to follow the laws of economic activity. It wouldn't be just to those who have loaned these sums not to be repaid." Economic laws harden inequalities developed in economic life. The biblical Jubilee was created so that every fiftieth year debt release would occur as part of a broad economic and community renewal. Slaves would be freed and poor people given a chance to start afresh, with equal access to the means of production.

When we press for more development aid for Africa, we're being partial. So, too, when we show compassion for those who suffer, for children growing up without parents, for communities devastated by AIDS and nations facing the crushing burden of debt payments, for farmers having to work depleted soil. All these require that the world take extraordinary steps, but only in this way will "deliverance to the needy" come.

If one is committed to preaching on the Gospel text, it is not as clear how to relate Matthew 3 to food and hunger concerns. Apart from John's call "Repent!" and his demand for deeds that prove one has repented, there aren't direct references to concern for poor and hungry people. Nor will John's image of the coming Messiah commend itself to most of us who can see how the actual Jesus clearly distanced himself from John's fiery preaching. For example, note how Jesus, in Luke 4:18-19, stopped his quote from Isaiah 61:1-2 short of the words "and the day of vengeance of our God."

If you must preach on a New Testament lection, Romans 15 provides better grist. Paul is writing about living in community, for Jews and Gentiles in the congregation in Rome. But apply this to other groups: First and Third World? Black and white? Paul lifts up hospitality themes. Is there a sermon here in which you compare being hospitable to others in our homes to showing hospitality more metaphorically? Whose food is it that we have in our storehouses? Is it all ours? Or is it food we have in stewardship from God? To whom do the benefits of technological advances belong? From whose inheritance do fossil fuel-based fertilizers come? To offer "hospitality" from our agricultural abundance may be a witness: "All good gifts around us are sent from heaven above." [1]

---

1. From refrain of "We Plow the Fields and Scatter," LBW 362.

Verse 15, a benediction, is designed to fill the Roman Christians with hope. God is "the God of hope." We certainly should understand that this offers us the prospect of life in God's wondrous reign. But we don't err if we look for a hope-referent in our earthly life, in historical time. Isn't what motivates the food and hunger activist the achievable vision of a qualitatively different world? A world where mothers don't have to watch their babes shrivel and die? A world where no one has written on her birth certificate "Destined not to thrive"?

Children's Time [LH]

God remembers people who are poor this time of year. There is a special place in God's heart for people who need food, clothing, a home, and who don't have enough money to pay all their bills. As we get closer and closer to Christmas, we think a lot about family and friends. Just as we care for those who are closest to us, God always cares for those who are forgotten. How can we do the same? Could we go to help in a soup kitchen, share some clothes, gather canned goods, offer toys to children who have none? This time of year reminds us that every day God asks us to remember those in need.

Musical Suggestions

Jesus Shall Reign Where'er the Sun—CH 95

Al Krass

Third Sunday of Advent

RCL: Isaiah 35:1-10; Psalm 146:5-10 or Luke 1:47-55; James 5:7-10; Matthew 11:2-11

LM: Isaiah 35:1-6a, 10; Psalm 146:6-7, 8-9, 9-10; James 5:7-10; Matthew 11:2-11

Over and over again in these Scriptures we see God's preferential option for poor and oppressed people. Though God is the Lord and Creator of the whole cosmos and has a special relationship with the descendants of Jacob, he also is one who "executes justice for the oppressed" and "gives food to the hungry" (Ps 146:7). He has a burden on his heart for prisoners and those who are blind and who are "bowed down" (under the weight of oppression?). He has a special concern for widows, orphans, and resident aliens. This is how his reign is identified.

The *Magnificat* in Luke, itself a psalm, is the alternative responsorial psalm. Mary, following Hannah (1 Sam 2:1-10), praises God for having entered history to overturn the world's power arrangements. It's those who are hungry and poor, God's lowly servants, who receive blessings, while the powerful are disestablished.

Isaiah, in wide-ranging prophetic imagery, expresses the same understanding of God. He paints a time and place that do not yet exist, when the full glory of God will be revealed. His conviction that such a time will come emboldens him to encourage those who suffer (35:3-4). Although they experience life as bitter, God will lift them up in full sight of their tormentors, radically changing their fortune. As they are redeemed, as God ransoms them out of captivity, they return to Jerusalem singing. The turnaround in their fortunes is so remarkable that Isaiah likens it to the blind seeing, the deaf hearing, the lame leaping, the mute singing. His picture includes a total renewal of nature!

The preacher who chooses this marvelous passage as the focus for a sermon needs to ask, "What images in today's world convey utter hopelessness?" A congested "badland" like the South Bronx? Undocumented immigrants working in sweatshops? Children in India, debt-slaves, working 14 hours a day making rugs? An Appalachian town with no employment and no medical care? Then go on to ask, "What would God's redemption of such places look like?" Finally, tie the two answers together by asking, "How does God in fact come to these marginalized sisters and brothers today?" Does God redeem them through action agencies against hunger? Through efforts to change government policy? By consumer boycotts? By labor or community organizing? How do Bread for the World's Offering of Letters campaigns fit in?

John the Baptist, as we saw last week, envisioned a Messiah very different from the one Jesus was. Imprisoned, he needs an answer to his nagging question: Is Jesus the promised Messiah? John sends his disciples to Jesus, who, aware of the differences between the two men, tells how they can determine whether God's reign is manifest in his ministry: by seeing what happens to the most helpless people! The Messiah, the bringer of God's redemption, will be known by his works, listed in verse 5 (works much like those described in Psalm 146). "The poor have good news brought to them" (Matt 11:5) is the final work and sums them all up. Jesus prays that John will be able to affirm this good news rather than be offended by his lack of "fire-and-brimstone preaching."

Today's preacher can surely ask if Jesus' response to John doesn't imply that for a church really to be the community of Christ, it must do works like he did. "If the poor were asked, 'Who are your friends?'"

President Julius Nyerere of Tanzania once asked a group of nuns, "are we so sure they would answer, 'The church'?"

Children's Time [LH]

Remind the children that when we're asked, "Who are you?" we usually answer with our names. (If there's time, go around and ask at least some of the children, "Who are you?") But if we go the next step, we can say more about ourselves: "I'm a student, a teacher, a brother or sister, a father or mother, a singer, a tennis player, a follower of Jesus." There are lots of ways we say who we are. In the Bible readings today, Mary and Jesus identify themselves as people who do things to help people by healing, feeding, caring for them. This is very good news! We can do those kinds of things too. Who do we say we are this season?

Musical Suggestions

Community of Christ—NCH 314

My Soul Gives Glory to My God—NCH 119

Al Krass

Fourth Sunday of Advent

RCL: Isaiah 7:10-16; Psalm 80:1-7, 17-19; Romans 1:1-7; Matthew 1:18-25

LM: Isaiah 7:10-14; Psalm 24:1-2, 3-4, 5-6; Romans 1:1-7; Matthew 1:18-24

The passage from Isaiah is a nest of problems. Cited in the Gospel because Matthew understands Isaiah 7:14 as a prophecy of Christ's birth to a virgin, the verses from Isaiah are about the conflict between King Ahaz of Judah and the prophet. Very little in the passage refers to the birth, and a majority of scholars agree that the young woman mentioned in verse 14, who was already pregnant, can't be identified with certainty. But the prophecy clearly concerned people and events occurring in Ahaz's time. Meaningful parallels often exist between what was once prophesied—and fulfilled—and situations in later times when God's similar actions are seen or are expected to take place.

One approach to preaching on the passage from Isaiah begins with God telling Isaiah to counsel King Ahaz that Jerusalem will not be overcome by the alliance between Israel and Syria and that the king just needs to trust God. Ahaz, however, refuses to trust, and instead decides to rely on a military response based on a risky political alliance. Isaiah begs him to simply ask God for a sign that Jerusalem is safe in God's hand. Ahaz, pretending to be a pious believer, declines to "put the Lord to the test." Isaiah testily responds that God will give him a sign anyway.

Now you're on the cusp of a challenging sermon! It's a sermon about war and peace. To be honest, a lot of the world's hunger problems arise because of war and its effects on farmers and displaced civilians. It's also true that solutions to world hunger are generally underfunded in part because so much of the nations' strength is used up in war-preparedness and warmaking. Isaiah suggests this is because of a lack of faith. If our U.S. leaders were persons of faith, would they choose military options the way they have? Would we have a $396 billion military budget when we can't even get $10 billion to fight world hunger? Remind the people that it is *our* representatives who vote for such policies. What does it say about our faith that we don't do more to challenge this? What does the sign of the babe born in Bethlehem say to us about all this?

Psalm 80 is a lament of a nation defeated in war—Israel—with a plea to be restored. Could you apply it to countries today that have been devastated by conflict? Psalm 24 could be used to preach about our stewardship of the world God has given us and the kind of lives God desires us to lead.

The passage from Romans revolves around verse 5: the purpose of God's sending Paul is "to bring about the obedience of faith among all the Gentiles." In the Today's English Version translation this verse reads: "in order to lead the people of all nations to believe and obey." We frequently downplay the ethical mandate in Christian preaching in favor of a supposed belief mandate. But, as Dietrich Bonhoeffer so memorably put it, "faith is only real when there is obedience, never without it, and faith only becomes faith in the act of obedience."[1] We dare not separate faith in Christ from our actions and our lives, which such faith entails. To "belong to Christ Jesus" is to be numbered among his "saints," working for the day when God's will "will be done," and God's "kingdom come on earth as it is in heaven." An interesting sermon might link Isaiah's urging Ahaz to have faith in God with the life in faith we're called to live as disciples of Christ.

It may be difficult to connect the Gospel's story of Joseph's faithfulness to God and to Mary with our activity today on behalf of the world's hungry people. The link that best lends itself to this purpose is the name Emmanuel, "God-with-us." What does it mean to say that the Christmas message of God being with us ends our time in the

1. Dietrich Bonhoeffer, *The Cost of Discipleship* (New York: Macmillan, 1979) 69.

wilderness, our time of being bereft? Psalm 80 may be what those who are bereft of God's presence pray. Because we know that God has drawn close to us in Christ and that our sins have been forgiven, are we then freed up to care for others?

Children's Time [LH]

Emphasize the theme of trust. Give examples from your own life or theirs when trust has been important or difficult or easy. Today's Bible lessons (Ahaz/Isaiah, Joseph) help us see that we can trust God to be God. Sometimes we worry that if we trust others, we may be let down if they aren't there to help us when we need it. God is one we can trust. How do we show others that we trust them and they can trust us?

Musical Suggestions

O Jesus, I Have Promised—NCH 493

God of Grace and God of Glory—NCH 436

Take My Life—CH 609

Al Krass

Christmas Eve

RCL: Isaiah 9:2-7; Psalm 96; Titus 2:11-14; Luke 2:1-14 (15-20)
LM: Isaiah 9:1-6; Psalm 96:1-2, 2-3, 11-12, 13; Titus 2:11-14;
Luke 2:1-14

Although the reading from Isaiah is chosen primarily because of verse 6, linger longer over the whole oracle —it has hidden treasures! Isaiah uses the "prophetic perfect" tense, speaking of things that haven't yet happened as if they've already taken place. You could describe his vision in shorthand: "David's Kingdom Is Restored to Full Glory." Look what the vision includes: light bursts forth; the nation is strengthened; joy increases; oppression ends; war is abolished; endless peace, justice, and righteousness come!

Translate this for your hearers by asking what they long for most. Some of the same things! Plus, some may yearn for an end to hunger, the wiping out of AIDS, an end to slavery, the restoration of blighted urban areas, an end to chemical dependency, teen-on-teen violence, and racism. Now, can you see these things as already present? Can you paint such a vivid picture of that for your congregation?

13

Then ask, How is this related to the Christ Child who has come to us? Does his coming give hope for a qualitatively different future? Can you call your people to renewed hope and to commit themselves to work for that new day? Edmund Sears does that in the latter verses of "It Came upon the Midnight Clear"—look at the hope he holds out for a coming golden age.

Psalm 96 is full of praise for God's establishing the earth and constantly bringing justice and equity. Though God has come and done this for ages, verse 13 tells us that there is still a greater coming to look for. What good news this is!

The passage from the letter to Titus is a real nugget, succinctly summarizing the Gospel. "The grace of God has appeared, bringing salvation to all" (v. 11), calling us to live properly in response. For our purposes, explore what verse 14 might mean for anti-hunger activists. What would it mean to be Christ's people, "zealous for good deeds"? What would be marks of a church like that?

The danger of the Lukan nativity passage is that it so easily becomes trite. Congregations are so cued in to its familiar words and cadences that it can become a numbing recitation. Here are some ideas to stir people to think:

1. Augustus's decree is for the empire's purposes, not the people's. It is a real burden to subject people.

2. The shepherds are terrified partly because, as uneducated, dirty, lowly, hired hands, they are not "into" religion. Yet the angels come to them, not to the priests or Pharisees. Amazingly, they are told that the Messiah enters human history in a position similar to theirs, with nowhere to sleep but in a feed-trough.

3. When the shepherds tell what they've learned, it blows people's minds (a loose translation of verse 18!). God isn't supposed to act this way!

4. Mary, who is held up as a model—as she should be for us too—is moved to a deep rethinking of what is going on, of how God acts, and of how she is involved.

Where does that lead you as you preach? Can you encourage your well-heeled suburban congregation to reassess its values? Can you help convince your congregation of self-deprecating "little people" to believe

God has specially chosen them? Can you witness to how you, as clergy, are shaken up by God's choice of shepherds as the medium of revelation?

Children's Time [LH]

It's very hard to keep children's attention at Christmas Eve services, and many pastors use stories to engage all age levels. If you do have a short children's time on Christmas Eve, have them think about how Jesus' coming changes things. The Bible shows us that no one is the same after Jesus comes. Here is a baby who promises peace, not war; health, not sickness; food, not hunger. Our happiness in seeing Jesus come is to think about changes he can bring in our lives. What are some of those changes? (Rather than have them shout out Christmas presents they hope to get, maybe suggest a few things they may hope for: better health for a relative, a visit from a friend or family member.)

Musical Suggestions

It Came upon the Midnight Clear—NCH 131

Al Krass

Christmas Day—Dawn

RCL: Isaiah 62:6-12; Psalm 97; Titus 3:4-7; Luke 2:(1-7) 8-20
LM: Isaiah 62:11-12; Psalm 97:1, 6, 11-12; Titus 3:4-7; Luke 2:15-20

As chapter 62 begins, Isaiah is unrepentant—he will not stop prodding and pestering God until the people's hopes are fulfilled, until Jerusalem is restored to its former glory. Their return to the Holy City has been a grave disappointment. Conditions are terrible. He posts sentinels to continually shout to God, day and night. It reminds me of the importunate widow in Luke, who keeps pestering the judge until her case is dealt with.

In verses 8-9 Isaiah reminds the people that this is not to ask anything from God but what God promised long ago: that laborers will regain claim to the whole harvest for which they labor. He encourages the people to claim that promise—indeed, in verses 10-12, to envision the promise as already fulfilled. Look at the names in verse 12 by which the people will now be known!

Can you help your congregation sense what it would mean for the poor farmers of the Mississippi Delta and Appalachia to find themselves "favored of God," "sought out," and "no longer forsaken"? Can you enable them to imagine how girls who dropped out of school when pregnant feel, after years of demeaning welfare and later requirements under the Temporary Assistance for Needy Families program, when they've attained their G.E.D. and have found self-respect as workers who receive a living wage? To be "the redeemed of the Lord" will for some mean becoming self-sufficient, for others being restored to health or working to recover from addiction. Many faith-based organizations testify how they have helped forsaken people experience God's love. Through education and mutual help programs, sometimes tied to Bible study programs and prayer groups, persons who once came as clients to soup kitchens and food cupboards now often staff these programs, sharing the good news of Christ with others.

Titus 3:4-7 are the words that persons who have experienced such redemption might express. Take some time to hear these words as a confession of faith by persons whom God has redeemed from a dreadful state. Verse 3 describes it in one way. Other descriptions might include how persons who now know themselves as believers, loved by God, once were people without any positive self-image. See 1 Peter 2:9-10. If you can hear these words as personal testimony, you also can hear them as the church's collective testimony about God's saving us through the birth of Christ. This is one way of understanding how "the goodness and loving kindness of God our Savior appeared" (v. 4).

Psalm 97 is a general hymn of praise to God. Notice who the God is who is praised: the God of justice and righteousness. That is why the psalmist says in verses 11-12 that this is a joyous revelation of God for those who are righteous. Perhaps we can see here an early form of Jesus' Beatitude: "Blessed are those who hunger and thirst for righteousness, for they will be filled" (Matt 5:6). Once again a dawn theme appears, ending a dark night.

Put together, these three readings give ample basis for a sermon focusing on the change from night to dawn in the coming of Christ. As we apply this to the kind of poverty- and hunger-related programs we advocate for, we could refer to them as being part of God's effort to bring in the dawn all over creation.

For notes on Luke 2, see Christmas Eve, pp. 14–15.

Children's Time [LH]

These readings promise wonderful goodness to many people. Name some of those people who are blessed in these passages. Name others in the congregation as well.

Musical Suggestions [LH]

Night of Silence—GC 342

When Christmas Morn Is Dawning—UMH 232

Break Forth, O Beauteous Heavenly Light—PH 26

Go Tell It on the Mountain—NCH 154

Al Krass

Christmas Day

RCL: Isaiah 52:7-10; Psalm 98; Hebrews 1:1-4 (5-12); John 1:1-14
LM: Isaiah 52:7-10; Psalm 98:1, 2-3, 3-4, 5-6; Hebrews 1:1-6;
   John 1:1-18 or 1:1-5, 9-14

Psalm 98, a great hymn of joy, easily applies to Christmas morning. The suggestions of nativity in it are: the making known of God's victory (vv. 2ff.) and the claim that the Lord "is coming to judge the earth" (v. 9). The Lord's judgment will be done with righteousness and to establish equity, which is in harmony with everything we affirm about the way God works when we seek, through our advocacy, to promote justice and equity. As we work, for example, to see immigrants receive full food stamp benefits and access to poverty-reduction programs, we serve the King, who will rule the world in justice. Like the physical world, we rejoice at our Lord's coming.

Today's readings bring us back to Second Isaiah, the prophet of the Exile. Israel is still in captivity in Babylon. Today's oracle promises deliverance. Those waiting in prison (52:2) are informed: you're going home! (The messenger who brings these welcome words is probably the prophet himself.) Chapter 40's reassuring words are fulfilled— Israel is comforted because she is freed, redeemed from prison. Like Israel, the entire earth will see that the God of Zion reigns.

What an opportunity this is to clarify why we engage in public witness. God's redemption takes place on a world-historical plane. We can't reduce the good news to personal testimony about the hearts of

19

individual believers. To say, "I've been saved by Christ" is to say, "The one who has saved me and other believers is the Lord who is about the business of remaking the world. He is Lord of all creation." We live in an interim time—between the rule of the world's powers and God's reign. In our hearts we've already enthroned Christ. The direction of God's salvation in Christ is toward his universal lordship.

Hebrews 1 is a beautiful paean of praise to just such a Son-born-to-be-ruler.

John's Prologue is rich with meaning, chiefly around the themes of light and life. There are many ways to connect those themes and the birth of Christ to the kind of work God wants us to do as we follow Christ. I will explore two:

- We live in a world of moral darkness, into which God has sent the light of Christ. A struggle goes on between the darkness and the light. The light is destined to enlighten everyone, but those who belong to the darkness still struggle to maintain their hegemony. When we call for food-justice and when we call for a radical change in society so that poverty will be eliminated, those who hold power don't willingly yield. Although we behave in nonviolent ways, we can't stop testifying. Until the darkness disappears and God's people live in the light, God will not rest—nor will we.

- The Son born into this world is the Word present with God at creation. Through him life has entered the world. Although one with God, he emptied himself (Phil 2:6-8) and "pitched his tent among us" (E.V. Rieu's literal translation of verse 14). The church that wants to identify with the Son needs to do the same: not to simply offer help from a dominant position above, but to identify with and live among the humble of the earth. To do this we may need to divest ourselves of our wealth, of our social privilege.

Years ago the congregation I served, which had just united with another church, responded to a request from the Red Cross to make its former sanctuary into a homeless shelter. It was Christmas Eve. I went to the 7-11 not far from that building, where my office still was, for a hot dog. I remarked to the woman behind the counter that for the first time since that structure was built, there would be no Christmas Eve service there. I told her why. "But isn't that what the Christmas story is all about, Pastor?" she replied.

Children's Time [LH]

Consider using the story told in the reflection above or another story from your own experience to illustrate what Christmas is all about. Remind the children that we often remember the traditions we have at Christmas that we observe year after year, but it's also the surprises that break into our lives that remind us what the season means.

Musical Suggestions [LH]

Joy to the World!—PH 40

From Heaven Above—PH 54

Born in the Night, Mary's Child—NCH 152

Al Krass

First Sunday after Christmas

RCL: Isaiah 63:7-9; Psalm 148; Hebrews 2:10-18; Matthew 2:13-23
  (or Epiphany readings)

LM: Sirach 3:2-6, 12-14; Psalm 128:1-2, 3, 4-5; Colossians 3:12-21 or
  3:12-17; Matthew 2:13-15, 19-23

Isaiah 63 expresses thanks for God's having redeemed Israel out of love and pity for God's people. The image of God "lifting them up and carrying them" is very touching. Often when we confront a situation of great tragedy, such as a famine or earthquake, we can do something like that. People in those situations often cannot even stand up—they must be lifted up and carried. Our connectedness to those in need, like God's compassion for us, moves us to intervene on their behalf.

Psalm 148 is one of the great praise-songs of Israel, with all creation praising God for its being and for redeeming God's people. Psalm 128 speaks of the assurance that comes to those who fear God and walk in God's ways.

The reading from Hebrews continues to speak of the incarnation, and here specifically about Christ entering flesh to do battle against the devil and free those enslaved to evil and death. (As we enter into the lives of others, do we become as one with them, and take risks that may be associated with that, or do we seek to help from a position of invulnerability?) The passage encourages trust in Jesus as "a merciful and faithful high priest," one who is anxious to help. The slavery image reminds us of the numbers of people still either literally or figuratively enslaved today and commends us to ask how God wants to help them. Microcredit programs, starting with the Grameen Bank in Bangladesh, offer poor people loans that provide them the opportunity to become independent of moneylenders to whom they have long been in virtual debt-slavery. With mercy God is seeing to the rapid expansion of these loan programs, administered by the vulnerable people of the world for and with one another. Whereas traditional credit only benefits those who are already economically in the mainstream, microcredit programs providing small-scale loans help poor people, especially women, get started on the path to economic self-sufficiency.

The passage from Colossians (vv. 12-17) is a wonderful catalogue of virtues motivating the people of God, the circulation system that keeps the Body of Christ alive and functioning. Can we understand these virtues not individualistically but as the virtues of the Body? What will it mean for us as Christ's church to "clothe" ourselves with compassion?

The Gospel is heavy indeed. The Holy Family's flight into Egypt is followed by the slaughter of the innocents. These themes are rehearsed in every annual report of relief and development agencies, in every publication of Bread for the World: insecure rulers misusing power, persecution and assassinations, parents mourning lost children, refugees fleeing to safety. Can we enable our congregations to understand the challenges many refugees and immigrants now in our country have faced, and ask what their unmet needs are? Can we help our people sympathize with the millions living in refugee camps around the world? Can we encourage our parishioners' gratitude for those countries willing to accept refugees, including many neighboring poor countries whose resources are strained to the limit by their hospitality? Can we point out the importance of the United Nations' refugee assistance programs? The preacher would do well to get the congregation to ask: Where is the Holy Family having to flee from today?

Children's Time [LH]

Have children tell you about times they've been "lifted up" and "carried." How did that feel for them? What new things did they see, and how did they feel secure in the hands of those who carried them? How does God help us by carrying us when we need it?

Musical Suggestions [LH]

Love Came Down at Christmas—UMH 242

In the Bleak Midwinter—UMH 221

Lord, I Lift Your Name on High—FWS 2088

Creating God—GC 580

Al Krass

Second Sunday after Christmas

RCL: Jeremiah 31:7-14 or Sirach 24:1-12; Psalm 147:12-20; Ephesians
  1:3-14; John 1:(1-9) 10-18

LM: Sirach 24:1-2, 8-12; Psalm 147:12-13, 14-15, 19-20; Ephesians
  1:3-6, 15-18; John 1:1-18

It's not surprising that many people
find activists like us "heavy." We're
good at painting pictures of injustice
and suffering. People rightly ask if
we ever have good news to proclaim.
Today's Scriptures are full of good
news! It's important that we learn the
lesson Jeremiah teaches: In the midst
of suffering, God gives a vision of what
comes after the suffering. Today's
passage, which comes before all have
been exiled to Babylon and elsewhere, is already about the joyful return from exile!

Jeremiah paints a beautiful picture. Can you imagine the procession? Listen to the people crying with joy! See the brooks of water
along which they walk. Imagine them singing aloud on Mount Zion.
Visualize the tables of grain, wine, and oil. Hear the sheep bleating.
See the young and the old dancing and making merry. (And watch the
clergy and lay people alike filling themselves up at the banquet!)

Think of the people in today's world whose lives have been decimated by years of famine and war. See those same people now living in abundance and peace. Third World countries have been given a fresh start, their indebtedness wiped out. Describe what universal education means. Picture children running off to school. Imagine mothers laughing, confident that their children will all survive, even while remembering the days when half the kids died before reaching the age of five. Whatever it is that service agencies have enabled your congregation to do, paint a picture of all that now completed! What do the farms look like? How do the people live? What does dignity look like? Paint this and say, "God has promised: it shall happen!" Psalm 147:13-14 provides such a picture of God's blessings for Israel.

One of my joys as a member of Old First Reformed United Church of Christ in Philadelphia is working with the family of Sam and Dorothy Juah, refugees who escaped from the Liberian civil war in the late 1990s and are now leaders in our church. It's encouraging to see their eight children—some biological and others adopted—growing up and participating in all parts of the church's mission. The Juahs know from painful experience—and remind us regularly—what great suffering they endured from war and tyranny, and later from their initial poverty in Philadelphia. But their joyous participation in God's mission now gives us even more confidence that God's deliverance is real. As the Juahs have been blessed, their family is now a blessing to many others.

The passage from Ephesians is also future-oriented. It tells of God's "plan for the fullness of time" (v. 10). As God promised, our destiny is to be Christ's full heirs. In the Holy Spirit we already have the pledge of our inheritance. As God's adopted children in Jesus, we're destined to "live for the praise of his glory" (v. 12), because God determined that we shall be redeemed. When God makes a commitment, God accomplishes it! Living in hope as we do is to have this confidence and, while we await its fulfillment, to be overflowing with praise, for we know God's already begun doing it. If we approached our work for justice and dignity with this kind of radiant hope, how different it might seem! Out of our anxiety we've been known to lay guilt on people. But Ephesians tells us not to be anxious but to abound in hope. If God has lavished on us the riches of his grace, we can be sure: God wants to lavish that on everyone.

For John 1:1-14, see the notes for Christmas Day (p. 20). The unique themes of today's longer passage, themes we might relate to the reading from Jeremiah, concern what we've received from Christ and how this gift has transformed our lives. We have received "power to become children of God" (v. 12) and "grace upon grace" from Christ's "fullness" (v. 16). The images are of abundance, especially abundant life. Bringing us abundant life is the reason for his coming (John 10:10). In contrast to Moses' gift, from Christ we've received grace and truth, not a list of oughts and shoulds. Receiving grace and truth is our gift of abundance from God.

In your sermon you might want to speak of our motivation for engaging in advocacy for those who are poor and hungry. It's not because of the requirements of the law that we do this, but because we are filled to overflowing with the grace we have received from God. We want to share it with everyone. We don't believe that God wants anyone who lives in creation to do without abundance.

Children's Time [LH]

Ask how many children have ever gone to a parade. Perhaps they remember something from the Fourth of July or another holiday or another procession. Perhaps the parade ended with a picnic or some other chance for people to share food. Have them recall the joy and excitement they felt. Remind them that God's people remembered with joy their love for Jerusalem when they came back after being far away for a long time. They probably didn't march back in a parade, but the same excitement we feel is like their joy in coming home. We're grateful for a God who brings us back home.

Musical Suggestions [LH]

We're Marching to Zion—SZ 3

You Are Our Living Bread—GC 819

You Are God's Work of Art—GC 810

Al Krass

Epiphany of the Lord

RCL: Isaiah 60:1-6; Psalm 72:1-7, 10-14; Ephesians 3:1-12; Matthew
2:1-12

LM: Isaiah 60:1-6; Psalm 72:1-2, 7-8, 10-11, 12-13; Ephesians 3:2-3a,
5-6; Matthew 2:1-12

Preaching on the Epiphany texts demands awareness of the various
times involved:

1. The time the prophets and the people looked forward to as a time
   of fulfillment.

2. The time of Jesus as a time of realization of prophetic testimony.

3. The time of the church—a time of *already* and a time of *not-yet*.

Then wrestle with these questions:

—How do I see the relationship of these various words to each of
these times and to our time in the twenty-first century?

—Was everything the prophets promised fulfilled in the Christ-event?
Or are some of those promises yet to be experienced?

—How do those to whom I preach understand the present time? What
does the Gospel say to them about the present and the future?

I believe the world has received a great revelation in the Christ-
event. Those of us blessed to be born after Christ's advent have heard

the good news, the mystery of God's working in Christ. We know how the story will turn out. But if we look at the hunger, sickness, oppression, poverty, and war remaining in our midst, we know that God isn't yet finished redeeming the world.

Isaiah 60 points in two directions: *back* to Christ's coming ("Your light has come, and the glory of the Lord has risen upon you" [v. 1], and nations have already "come to [Israel's] light, and kings to the brightness of [its] dawn" [v. 3]); and *forward* to the fulfillment of these promises (after darkness covers the earth, "the Lord will arise upon you" [v. 2], and "You shall see and be radiant; your heart shall thrill and rejoice" [v. 5]).

Similarly, I rejoice reading Psalm 72. When I sing Isaac Watts's paraphrase in "Jesus Shall Reign," I believe Watts is right: Christ is the king Israel was told to hope for. For more comments on Psalm 72, see the Second Sunday of Advent (pp. 4–5).

Reading that the Magi "knelt down and paid [Christ] homage" with gold, frankincense, and myrrh, we know that that event was foretold and has already happened. It is, however, only a foretaste of the universal reign of Christ. Today's global church is further fulfillment of that promise. God is working his purpose out: to bring all nations in one body to the praise of God's glory. But there's more future in that still waiting to happen.

So when I regard the terrible conditions under which the world's poor people live, I am both challenged and comforted. I'm challenged to become, like Paul, "a servant [of this gospel] according to the gift of God's grace" (Eph 3:7). I'm comforted to know God's eternal purpose: that the whole world shall know the mystery of Christ, that all shall benefit from his promise. This is the most inclusive vision possible. No one is excluded!

The Magi, when they see that the star has stopped, are "overwhelmed with joy." *Our* promise, they were saying, has been fulfilled! I take that promise to include not just spiritual blessings but very material ones that are part of Christ's universal lordship. They've started to take place now—we're involved in God's work for them as advocates and activists. Psalm 72 offers the glimpse: there will be justice and equity; the cause of poor people will be defended; needy ones will be delivered; all oppressors will be crushed; the lives of the weak will be saved; and violence will end. There will also be "abundance of grain in the land"!

Children's Time [LH]

The Magi brought gifts worthy of a king, but Jesus wasn't found in a palace. If we think about things to bring as gifts to a child who isn't rich, what would we bring? Today, in our nation and even our own town or city, children need our help. The Magi remind us that bringing gifts doesn't end on Christmas Day. We thank God and others by offering gifts every day.

Musical Suggestions [LH]

Jesus Shall Reign—NCH 300

What Gift Can We Bring—UMH 87

Brightest and Best—NCH 156, 157

In a Lowly Manger Born—NCH 162

Arise, Your Light Is Come—NCH 164

David Beckmann

Baptism of the Lord

RCL: Isaiah 42:1-9; Psalm 29; Acts 10:34-43; Matthew 3:13-17
LM: Isaiah 42:1-4, 6-7; Psalm 29:1-2, 3-4, 3, 9-10; Acts 10:34-38;
    Matthew 3:13-17

John's baptism of Jesus and the proclamation of Christ as the beloved Son of God establish Jesus as the broker of God's reign on earth. In our own baptism we turned away from sin, and God called us as beloved children. Our self-centered identities were drowned, and we were raised out of the water as agents of God's kingdom.

In Isaiah 42 we get a clear picture that justice and righteousness are key aspects of God's kingdom. God's justice is rooted in lifting up those who are oppressed and marginalized: those in prison, those who are blind, those in darkness. For the biblical audience, opening blind people's eyes is not simply a miraculous physical healing. In those times people with disabilities or disease were outcasts who were rejected from society and considered sinners. As God opens blind people's eyes and releases prisoners, God is also restoring right relationships among people, lifting up the downtrodden and returning them to wholeness in community. The Lord has taken us by the hand and called us to be instruments of justice and righteousness.

Peter confirms Jesus' justice mission in Acts 10, as he preaches peace through Jesus and tells the story of Jesus "doing good and healing all who were oppressed" (v. 38). Peter issues a broad invitation to God's kingdom. God's justice-reign includes all people, Jews and Gentiles, sinners alike, calling us all to lives of fullness, freed from sin, loved by God. Peter preaches that all can be baptized and receive forgiveness of sins through Jesus' name. In turn, we then share the good news of God's forgiveness, of the new relationship we enjoy with God and one another, and of God's coming kingdom among us.

Some biblical images for God's kingdom, like blind people seeing or a lion lying with the lamb, seem impossible. But in baptism we have experienced some of the impossible becoming possible as our sins are forgiven and strangers become sisters and brothers.

The Bible often compares God's kingdom to a banquet or makes sharing food a means of filling deep hunger (Matt 14:13-21; Matt 22:1-14). God clearly intends for all people to have enough to eat. When people in our neighborhoods and around the world are hungry, we cannot claim we are in right relationship with them. One way we live out our baptism and share the good news of God's kingdom is by helping struggling people get enough to eat.

Ending world hunger may seem to be one of those impossible dreams. Yet in fact God graciously has given to humanity in our time the technology and resources to end widespread hunger. Stronger commitment from our nation's people and government are pivotal in making progress against hunger in our own country and worldwide. We can take part in hunger ministries in our community and support church-sponsored development programs in poor countries. We can also urge our elected representatives to ensure that the U.S. government does its part by providing hungry families with assistance and opportunity.

We are baptized into children of God. Tackling the problem of world hunger is not too much for us.

Children's Time [LH]

Take the children to the place where baptisms are done in the church. Show them the water and remind them that Jesus was baptized, and so were we. Ask what they remember about baptisms they've seen in church. Being baptized changes us and says to the world that we are God's children. That means that other people are our sisters and brothers in God's eyes—people in our congregation and around the world—and so we care for them, especially when they need food and shelter. Water can do amazing things!

Musical Suggestions [LH]

Wade in the Water—CH 371

Now the Silence—UMH 619

Breathe on Me, Breath of God—BP 88

God Has Chosen Me—GC 682

David Beckmann

Second Sunday in Ordinary Time

RCL: Isaiah 49:1-7; Psalm 40:1-11; 1 Corinthians 1:1-9; John 1:29-42
LM: Isaiah 49:3, 5-6; Psalm 40:2, 4, 7-8, 8-9, 10; 1 Corinthians 1:1-3;
   John 1:29-34

Both the Old and New Testaments are brimming with examples of
how God uses ordinary people to accomplish extraordinary things.
God calls us all, regardless of the ability we perceive in ourselves, to do
God's work. Through us God can accomplish miracles.

Isaiah says that the Servant was called to God's work before birth.
God has plans for us even in the womb. It is amazing that God has
involved us *at all* in bringing about God's purposes on earth. Even we
sinners—all of us—have roles to play.

We see this point illustrated in John's version of Jesus' calling his
first disciples, including Andrew and Simon Peter. These two are fishermen, poor, and likely not men of power and status. They aren't kings
or priests or rabbis; they are simply people whom Jesus calls to do
God's work.

Understanding that God has purpose and plans for every person
makes it even more heart-rending that so many people in our world
are debilitated or die of hunger and hunger-related diseases. Surely
this is not what God desires for their lives. God's plans for us may well
include a role in changing the world so that hungry people will have
enough to eat.

Some of us are led to ministries, like working in soup kitchens or
food shelves, which deal with immediate needs. Others are called to

tutor a child or help with a community organization. And some are pulled toward dealing with root causes of hunger through advocacy and lobbying members of Congress about hunger issues.

When a person responds to God's beckoning, amazing things can happen. A few years ago Pat Pelham of Birmingham, Alabama, heard a call from God to somehow respond to Africa's needs. It led her to get involved in Bread for the World. She and others spoke to their representative in Congress, a conservative Republican named Spencer Bachus, about debt relief for the world's poorest countries. They convinced him to work for debt relief and for policies that would direct the money that countries would have spent on debt repayment toward services for poor people. Representative Bachus was moved by the group and became a leading and effective advocate for debt relief.

Thousands of Christians and other people of goodwill around the world worked for debt relief for the poorest countries, many as part of the ecumenical Jubilee 2000 campaign. Because of debt relief, more children are now in school and more medicines are in rural clinics in some of the world's poorest countries. And it probably wouldn't have happened without the leadership of Representative Bachus and, before that, the active faith of Pat Pelham.

Pat and her friends didn't feel that they had any special talent when they went to speak to Representative Bachus, but they did have a conviction that our powerful government should do more to provide help and opportunity to poor and hungry people worldwide. Their conviction swayed Representative Bachus. And God clearly used them!

A part of this week's readings that really struck me was the reference in 1 Corinthians 1:5 to knowledge and speech. Paul later in the letter criticizes the people in the Corinthian church for how they use these gifts. But Bread for the World helps people use their gifts of speech and knowledge to help hungry people. We learn about the underlying causes of hunger (partly by reading Bread for the World materials), and we then speak to others in our churches and to our representatives in Congress about government policies that can give hungry families a better chance to provide for themselves.

Children's Time [LH]

Remind the children of times when we play games and choose people to be on our teams. We choose people because they play the game well—if it's baseball, because they can hit the ball or can throw well; or if it's basketball, because they can shoot baskets. This week and next, the Bible stories include Jesus' calling his disciples to follow him. Jesus chose disciples because he needed them to do things—to go out and tell others the good news that he brought and to do good things for others. The disciples were ordinary people like us, but Jesus asked them to join him to do some pretty awesome tasks. Jesus invites us to follow him too—to share God's love with others.

Musical Suggestions [LH]

I, the Lord of Sea and Sky (Here I Am, Lord)—BP 129

The Summons—FWS 2130

We Are Called—GC 718

Lord, Whose Love in Humble Service—LBW 423

David Beckmann

▪

Third Sunday in Ordinary Time

▪

RCL: Isaiah 9:1-4; Psalm 27:1, 4-9; 1 Corinthians 1:10-18; Matthew 4:12-23

LM: Isaiah 8:23–9:3; Psalm 27:1, 4, 13-14; 1 Corinthians 1:10-13, 17; Matthew 4:12-23 or 4:12-17

The passage from Isaiah starts with the anguish of Israel's northern tribes, Zebulun and Naphtali. Assyria had conquered them, but Isaiah promises great liberation to this oppressed people. Light will come to people who walk in darkness. God "will make glorious the way of the sea, the land beyond the Jordan, Galilee of the nations" (v. 1).

Most of Jesus' ministry was in this same area, then the province of Galilee, and Matthew sees this as a fulfillment of Isaiah's prophetic promise. Galilee included many Gentiles, and Jerusalem's priestly class took a dim view of the beliefs and practices of many Galilean Jews. But Jesus began his preaching and healing among this "people who walked in darkness" (v. 2).

Jesus then calls fishermen to be his first disciples. Fishermen are poor. But Jesus chooses those who have little. God chooses them—and us—though we are unlikely saints. God often starts at the margins. People on the margins of society and people who have little are sometimes more open to the Spirit than people who have much.

Paul reminds the Corinthians that God's decisive revelation was Christ's suffering and death on the cross. Jesus became a helpless outcast. It makes no sense for us to be proud or stand-offish when we have been baptized into the way of the cross. We expect to find God Almighty amidst indignity and suffering.

A woman I know named Patricia Edwards is an example of an unlikely person God has asked to make a difference. Poor and a single mom on welfare, Patricia didn't seem like the kind of person who had much to offer. Her minimum wage and temporary jobs weren't even enough to make ends meet and put food on the table for her four growing boys. But with assistance from her state's welfare program, Patricia began to take classes at a local community college to gain the education she needed to secure long-term, stable employment. In the midst of her study, Patricia also became involved in programs to help other poor families get the education needed for gainful employment. Her work helped change laws in her state so that more adults on welfare could go to school and, with a college degree, escape poverty for good.

Patricia's story illustrates that even people whom society often deems unworthy of praise (fishermen, tax collectors, poor people, mothers who receive welfare) can be agents of God's justice and love.

Do we know people with special needs who are also especially active in God's service? Have times of trouble made us more open to God and ready to help others? How is God calling us to give up some of our comfort and status to follow Christ?

Do we know families who sometimes struggle to put food on the table? How do they experience God? If we don't know such families, are we missing out on important aspects of what God is doing in our own community?

Children's Time [LH]

Before the worship service, think of someone in your own life who has made an impact on you or others but who was not someone of power and prestige. Perhaps it is someone who struggled against odds or overcame personal or societal barriers to change lives. Share the story with the children to encourage them to be open to how unexpectedly we may be blessed by those whose "credentials" are often undervalued.

Musical Suggestions [LH]

We'll Walk No Longer in the Darkness—BP 199

Take Up Your Cross, the Savior Said—PH 393

In Christ There Is No East or West—UMH 548

Jesus Calls Us—UMH 398

David Beckmann

Fourth Sunday in Ordinary Time

RCL: Micah 6:1-8; Psalm 15; 1 Corinthians 1:18-31; Matthew 5:1-12

LM: Zephaniah 2:3; 3:12-13; Psalm 146:6-7, 8-9, 9-10; 1 Corinthians
1:26-31; Matthew 5:1-12a

The passages from Micah and Zephaniah are clear about what God wants of us: humility, kindness, and justice. The passage from Micah tells how the Lord rescued his people from slavery and wandering in the desert. They owe more to God than animal sacrifices, more even than the sacrifice of their own children. What God requires is nothing less than their own hearts and lives. Zephaniah prophesies destruction and terror but believes that these, too, are ways that the Lord brings people to humility, obedience, and justice.

Psalm 146 is a wonderful complement to these passages from the prophets. The psalm praises the Lord for executing justice for the oppressed, giving food to hungry people, and upholding widows and orphans. The justice, kindness, and humility that the Lord requires of us are reflections of the Lord's own character.

Jesus reiterates the prophets' message in the Beatitudes, but in an especially demanding way. God offers blessing to those who are poor in spirit and who are meek to the point of mourning. God requires us to seek justice with a passion—and suffer for it. The Beatitudes make most Christians cringe. Those of us who live in comfort in the world's wealthy countries are not the meek of the earth; few of us suffer all that much for justice. In fact, I think we can only bear to listen to the

Beatitudes with an open heart because it is Jesus who is talking to us. We know that Jesus loves us and will not reject us because we fall short.

Jesus' own life and death embody the Beatitudes. His death on the cross is kindness in the extreme. Rather than imposing God's will on the world, as people expected a messiah to do, Jesus forgives those who plotted against him and submits to suffering and death at their hands.

God then raises Jesus from the dead, as evidence that Jesus is indeed the Christ. By faith in him, we experience Jesus' forgiveness for our own sins. As Paul explains to the Corinthians, Jesus' cross is the basis for a Christian's relationship with God. The experience of God's forgiveness in Jesus Christ moves us to express some of his self-giving Spirit in our own lives.

The whole Bible, from Genesis to Revelation, tells us that God is self-emptying and loving. In God's embrace, we become more generous and committed to justice ourselves.

Children's Time [LH]

In advance, make a list of the ways your church embodies the three facets of Micah's charge, including programs children and adults take part in. Point out to the children that the Bible makes clear that loving God means more than going to church each Sunday. Worshiping God is important, but our faith is active in other ways too. Tell them about how the items on your list witness to the humble, caring, and justice-oriented work God calls us to do.

Musical Suggestions [LH]

We Are Called—GC 718

What Does the Lord Require—UMH 441

O God of Love, O King of Peace—LBW 414

All Who Love and Serve Your City—BP 165

David Beckmann

Fifth Sunday in Ordinary Time

RCL: Isaiah 58:1-9a (9b-12); Psalm 112:1-9 (10); 1 Corinthians 2:1-12
  (13-16); Matthew 5:13-20

LM: Isaiah 58:7-10; Psalm 112:4-5, 6-7, 8-9; 1 Corinthians 2:1-5;
  Matthew 5:13-16

At Bread for the World, we use the passage from Isaiah about false and true worship quite often to describe why Christians should be about the business of ending hunger. Piety and praying, by themselves, don't get to the root of God's kingdom of justice and righteousness. God requires action that makes God's reign real: release captives, free oppressed people, feed those who are hungry, house homeless people, provide clothes for those who are naked. God promises to reward charity and justice with God's own guidance, presence, and blessing.

The salt and light passage in Matthew is also a call to action. Salt is useless if it doesn't enhance the taste of food, and light does no good unless it lights up the world around it. Faith is useless if it doesn't somehow change the world.

We are called to manifest God's glory by acting for God's kingdom here and now, proclaiming justice and righteousness. For this reason, Christians work to end hunger and poverty, rebuild broken relationships, bring peace and reconciliation, bind up those who are brokenhearted, and support the sick and weak ones among us. In so doing, we can help reveal God's goodness in this world.

Paul reminds the Corinthians that lofty words are not what characterize his preaching, but rather the conviction and wisdom that comes from the Spirit. The Spirit directs us to deploy our gifts, not for self-aggrandizement but rather for service.

Some people are less effective than they might be because they underestimate their gifts and God's intentions for them. In her book *A Return to Love,* Marianne Williamson writes:

> Our deepest fear is not that we are inadequate. Our deepest fear is that we are powerful beyond measure. It is our light, not our darkness, that most frightens us. We ask ourselves, who am I to be brilliant, gorgeous, talented and fabulous? Actually, who are you not to be? You are a child of God. Your playing small does not serve the world. There's nothing enlightened about shrinking so that other people won't feel insecure around you. We are all meant to shine, as children do. We were born to make manifest the glory of God that is within us. It's not just in some of us; it's in everyone. And as we let our own light shine, we unconsciously give other people permission to do the same. As we're liberated from our own fear, our presence automatically liberates others.[1]

God has given every person unique gifts and calls us all to be salt and light for the world. We shouldn't underestimate our gifts but deploy them for God's purposes.

Children's Time [LH]

Bring some salt with you and invite one child to hold out a hand, and you pour salt in it (check first with parents to ensure they agree to this). Ask the child if the salt smells (no) or has an attractive color (no).

1. Marianne Williamson, *A Return to Love: Reflections on the Principles of Course of Miracles* (New York: HarperCollins, 1992) 165.

Then ask the child to taste it, and point out that salt can dramatically change the taste of soup or other foods. It doesn't take much to make a big difference. Point out that the small things we do to help others and serve God also make a lot of difference.

Musical Suggestions [LH]

Gather Us In—GC 744

What is Salt Without Its Flavor?—BP 194

Bring Forth the Kingdom—GC 658

We Utter Our Cry—UMH 439

The Reverend Canon Saundra D. Richardson

◼

Sixth Sunday in Ordinary Time

◼

RCL: Deuteronomy 30:15-20; Psalm 119:1-8; 1 Corinthians 3:1-9;
Matthew 5:21-37

LM: Sirach 15:15-20; Psalm 119:1-2, 4-5, 17-18, 33-34; 1 Corinthians
2:6-10; Matthew 5:17-37 or 5:20-22a, 27-28, 33-34a, 37

Deuteronomy 30:15-20 and the appointed verses of Psalm 119 center
on walking in God's way, following the commandments, choosing life.
The reading from Matthew focuses on how we can miss walking in
God's way even when we are legalistically compliant. Jesus' new appli-
cation of the law shows that not following the commandments can
result in injustice to others. The verses then describe what we should
do to be reconciled in these situations.

The passage from Corinthians regarding division in the church causes
us to pause and ponder. We ask, "Who has planted and watered us?"
The season of Epiphany celebrates Christ's light in the world. In that
celebration are thoughts of birth and life, and we remember people
who have been the light of the world for us. Mothers give us birth, and
along life's journey many people have a hand in shaping who we are.
Our life experiences and the people involved in those moments prepare us for the next stage and nurture us into the persons that we are
and can become. Think of persons who have made a difference in your
own life, each seeming to build on the other's work preparing your life,
your soul, your soil for the next step. Give examples in the sermon.

As God causes us to grow from planted and watered seeds, how
do we respond to these gracious, nurturing acts, following God's

commandments? We are not alone in seeking a justice-oriented response to God's goodness. We can work together with ecumenical/interfaith partners to make a difference in our community, nation, and world. We can make decisions, even in our fractured world, so that all may eat, have adequate healthcare, jobs, housing, education, and public transportation. The church can be an agent to fulfill God's yearning that all creation enjoy fullness of life.

How can ecumenical partners make a difference in our communities and nurture our youth? Nowadays people come to our church doors asking for food, needing help with utilities and rent, and hoping to secure jobs. Children go to school hungry. Employers sometimes see employees stealing food to take home.

Food pantries often become the quick fix and in some ways are the simplest congregational response. But don't stop there! Many churches now have varied ministries, including soup kitchens, food pantries, walk-in ministries, and health clinics working separately or together with other groups to meet people's needs. Often these efforts are linked with advocacy, as people speak out to elected leaders about longer-term remedies. Explore other challenging ways to provide opportunities for people to improve their life situations.

Paul's image in Corinthians of planting and watering inevitably brings gardening to mind. Some in your congregation may now be planning their spring gardens. Two opportunities for your church come to mind—a community garden and a training center. Both can help people "fish for life" to improve their situations.

Community gardens provide an intergenerational opportunity for different denominations, ethnic groups, and vocations to work together. It will be a hands-on experience and training ground for those in need to enhance their quality of life. And it's a plus for the look of the neighborhood. To begin, church members may own vacant lots near communities of need, or your town or city may have publicly owned vacant land. With a plan and design in hand, many people can play a role by plowing and tilling; raising funds to purchase seeds and seedlings; planting, weeding, hoeing, watering, harvesting, sharing recipes, and teaching how to can, freeze, or preserve the bounty. Canning and freezing offers abundance beyond the harvest. Working in the soil provides a learning opportunity that nurtures not only the plants, but also one's self.

The passage from Corinthians (v. 9) not only suggests that we are God's field but also God's building. Perhaps there is a vacant building a church member or your town or city owns that can be purchased or leased for a training center. Renovating the building could be a training experience for those in the community seeking skills toward employability and self-sufficiency. The training center can become a place for persons to learn computer skills, basic literacy, and culinary skills, and to obtain a GED. The center could also house a daycare center not only for the persons going through training but also for parents in the vicinity so that they can work. This can be a tangible sign that others care for them and in turn can increase their self-esteem.

Other challenges could take your congregation even further, into the issues of adequate and affordable housing and working for living wages and health insurance for local workers. Perhaps there is a proposal before the community that you could emphasize, something on an upcoming ballot or on the agenda of your local, state, or national legislature. This may also be a good time to plan for Bread for the World's annual letter-writing campaign to Congress or to highlight recent correspondence from your denomination's Washington office.

Children's Time

Talk about their families and friends and how they have learned from one another. Ask how they help other people. What do they know about sharing and caring for one another? Ask who has helped them in their lives and how. Share experiences of your childhood.

Musical Suggestions

Father, we thank thee who has planted—EH 302, 303

There's a wideness in God's mercy—EH 470

Open your ears, O faithful people—EH 536

I want to walk as a child of the light—EH 490

We plow the fields and scatter—EH 291

We All Are One in Mission—PH 435

The Reverend Canon Saundra D. Richardson

Seventh Sunday in Ordinary Time

RCL: Leviticus 19:1-2, 9-18; Psalm 119:33-40; 1 Corinthians 3:10-11,
16-23; Matthew 5:38-48
LM: Leviticus 19:1-2, 17-18; Psalm 103:1-2, 3-4, 8, 10, 12-13;
1 Corinthians 3:16-23; Matthew 5:38-48

God calling us to help one another walk in God's way is an over-
arching theme in these readings, following from last week's lessons.

The reading from 1 Corinthians reminds us that God's temple and
Spirit are in us, the Church. The same sense echoes in the reading from
Leviticus, which directs each of us to be holy, reflecting God's holiness.

How do we let God's Spirit in us come to the surface? In our busy,
results-driven world, we might think direct action is the best way. But
don't miss opportunities to experience some silence each day and to
take quiet days and retreats. Your sermon might talk of how cell phones,
beepers, and e-mail have robbed us of precious time for silence.

Howard Thurman's *The Inward Journey* speaks about silence. "[I]t
is out of the silence that all sound comes; it is in the stillness that the
word is fashioned for the meaning it conveys. Here the sound without
sounds can be most clearly heard and meanings out of which all values
come can be plumbed." [1]

It is in and with the silence that God can speak to us of what is
needed to be holy and to share wholeness with those who are broken.
Through silence and reflection, we are more apt to hear God and open

1. Howard Thurman, *The Inward Journey* (Richmond, Ind.: Friends United Press,
1971) 53.

our eyes to the world around us. Thus grounded, action can be started and sustained. Give examples of opening our eyes to the surrounding neighborhood or larger community in ways that allow us to recognize previously unseen needs and advocate appropriate solutions.

Leviticus 19 connects holiness and sharing with those in need. "You shall be holy, for I the Lord your God am holy. . . . you shall not reap to the very edges of your field. . . . You shall not strip your vineyard bare, or gather the fallen grapes of your vineyard; you shall leave them for the poor and the alien" (vv. 2, 9, 10).

I remember growing up in East Tennessee next to a county where a national canning company was located. When the canning company opened its fields to the public after harvesting, my mother and others would go to the fields to pick green beans, greens, tomatoes, and other vegetables. This food helped supplement what we grew in our own garden and the non-vegetable government commodities we received. My mother and others canned and froze the bounty from the cannery's fields, which helped us through the winter.

Remind the congregation how delighted we are when work colleagues or neighbors share extra vegetables from their bumper crops. They are proud of what they have grown and do not want to see the vegetables go to waste. Often these gleanings are left in the common rooms or kitchens at work or near the sidewalk or curb in our neighborhoods, free for the taking. Since vegetable gardening is not as common as it was decades ago, we appreciate these gifts even more. There's nothing like homegrown tomatoes and cucumbers!

But reflect a moment. Should it always be the *extra* that's given, or does God's generous spirit challenge us to give *before* there is extra? What are the deeper issues at stake? For example, how do our nation's policies make it harder for black farmers in the South and family farmers in our agricultural heartland to keep their lands and continue growing food and strengthening our nation's rural economy? In our own areas, how do we find ways to teach, to give opportunities so that people can learn to provide for themselves? How do we give such opportunities in today's economic system? Explore whether locally owned companies provide opportunities for vulnerable people to learn skills and whether they provide affordable or on-site daycare and adequate health insurance for their employees.

How can we support educational opportunities to keep kids in school through high school so that they have employable skills? How can we teach and model to teenagers that there's more to life than sexual activity and drugs? Share examples of how your congregation may want to partner with schools and community groups for after-school programs.

Might all these be ways we testify to God's Spirit dwelling in us and examples of how we seek to be holy as God is holy?

Children's Time

Talk about silence. What do you hear in the silence? Talk of how God sometimes comes in the silence to help us do what is needed. You may also ask about sharing toys or snacks with a friend and ask what they do when a friend or family member is sad or hurt. How do those actions show others that we love God because God has been good to us?

Musical Suggestions

Now the silence—EH 333

Songs of thankfulness and praise—EH 135

I want to walk as a child of the light—EH 490

Lord, you give the great commission—EH 528

O Zion, haste—EH 539

We Are Marching in the Light of God (Siyahamb')—NCH 526

Eighth Sunday in Ordinary Time

RCL: Isaiah 49:8-16a; Psalm 131; 1 Corinthians 4:1-5; Matthew 6:24-34
LM: Isaiah 49:14-15; Psalm 62:2-3, 6-7, 8-9; 1 Corinthians 4:1-5;
Matthew 6:24-34

God cares deeply for creation, and we can trust God fully in that care. Isaiah's Jubilee theme is very clear. God covenants not only "to establish the land [and] apportion the desolate heritages" (v. 8), but God also offers release to prisoners, light to those in darkness, food and water to those who hunger and thirst. "The Lord has comforted his people, and will have compassion on his suffering ones" (v. 13).

Matthew 6 and Psalm 62 call us to not be anxious and to trust God. The passage from Matthew was a reading for Morning Prayer in the first week of a two-week silent retreat I attended at Emery House of St. John the Evangelist in West Newbury, Massachusetts. The hermitage has a sunroom with long windows looking out into the woods. If I put my rocking chair just right, I could look to the right and see the Artichoke River and to the left the Merrimac River, much farther away.

In the silence of the late April days preceding this reading, I observed the birds, squirrels, tall trees, and geese, and noticed the greening of plants and trees. There were several rainy and windy days during which I noticed the very tall trees bending and swaying. I thought of their pliability and how they did not break.

On one of these days, I read about bending from Howard Thurman's *Deep Is the Hunger*. Thurman talks about trees bending to have life,

51

sustained by the sturdy growth from which they come. "The tree seems to say to the branches, 'Bend with the wind but do not release your hold, and you can ride out any storm.'"[1] Thurman explores how this image relates to compromise in human life. He says: "A man does not make a compromise in a given situation; he merely adjusts. . . . A careful examination of any man's life would reveal that, at one point he bends with the wind and keeps on living, while at another point he defies the wind and is quite prepared to be brought crashing to the ground."[2]

Tall trees are pliable and adjust to the wind. Animals have survival instincts that are very strong. These seem to be more innate to nature than humanity. Is it the anxiety chemicals in our systems that cause us to not be pliable and bend with less anxiety?

I pondered God's making animal and plant life and how dependent they are on each other. Walks through nearby Maudsley State Park exhibited so much coming to life as God's creation celebrated spring. As the weeks went by, more life would appear, and then it would be fall and resting time for many plants and vegetation. Yet winter is the heyday for the firs and other evergreen trees and plants.

Birds and squirrels take pollen and seeds to other places, providing growth and fertilization that ultimately provides food for other creatures. All that the squirrels and birds needed was there for them. They didn't worry. They scampered from tree to tree and through the woods in the fullness of life. Baby squirrels were learning to make their way. If God was taking care of them, why was I to worry so about my own life?

Examples of some questions to explore are:

• How do we learn to make our way?

• How do we help others to make their way and provide for them?

• How do we show others to make their way?

• How do we find ways to lessen their worries and our worries?

As we observe animals meeting their needs from their surroundings, how can we better use the God-given abilities, talents, and resources

---

1. Howard Thurman, *Deep Is the Hunger* (Richmond, Ind.: Friends United Press, 1978) 12.
2. Ibid., 13, 14.

of a wealthy nation so that no person in our community is hungry, that there is adequate healthcare, insurance, and medicines, adequate housing and jobs, and a decent quality of life? Share examples of how this is happening in your community and how members of your church are involved.

Ask questions about times when people have been anxious. Share some examples from your own life and from anxious times that the congregation has experienced. Encourage the congregation to reflect on how particular people affected their lives when they were worried, anxious, down and out. How did that make a difference? Give examples of how to transfer this to an awareness of others' needs and a willingness to help them.

Children's Time

Talk about nature—plants and animals. If this is a community without a lot of wooded areas, then refer to a park or wooded area that they might know. Ask how they see squirrels, birds, and rabbits getting food in their yards. Talk about how God takes care of nature, how plentiful food is provided, how rain helps growth, the need for sunlight.

Ask them about how they learned to ride a bike, swim, etc., and the anxieties they may have experienced. Let them share how they became less anxious.

Musical Suggestions

I want to walk as a child of the light—EH 490

Christ, whose glory fills the skies—EH 7

Morning has broken—EH 8

Not here for high and holy things—EH 9, vv. 1, 4, 5, 6

Holy Spirit, ever living—EH 511

Come down, O love divine—EH 516

Surely it is God who saves me—EH 678, 679

If the choir has Jack Noble White's "The First Song of Isaiah," that could be sung with the congregation doing the refrains.

The Reverend Canon Saundra D. Richardson

Transfiguration of the Lord

RCL: Exodus 24:12-18; Psalm 2 or Psalm 99; 2 Peter 1:16-21;
Matthew 17:1-9

LM: Daniel 7:9-10, 13-14; Psalm 97:1-2, 5-6, 9; 2 Peter 1:16-19;
Matthew 17:1-9

In some faith traditions, the Transfiguration accounts occur on the last Sunday of Epiphany and on August 6 as the Feast of the Transfiguration. In the Episcopal Church, the readings from Exodus and Matthew are for the last Sunday of Epiphany in Year A with Philippians 3:7-14. The Lukan account of the Transfiguration (Luke 9:28-36) is used for August 6 along with Exodus 34:29-35 and 2 Peter 1:13-21. Since August 6 only occurs occasionally on a Sunday, the last Sunday of Epiphany allows those who attend weekday Eucharist to hear the Transfiguration themes twice in a year.

All three appointed lessons are mountaintop experiences, and the psalm reflects the might, majesty, and glory of God on high. In Exodus, Moses goes on the mountaintop for forty days and nights to receive the tablets of the commandments. Psalm 99 recounts the Lord's speaking to Moses, Aaron, and Samuel out of the pillar of cloud.

Matthew tells of Jesus' transfiguration on the mountain in the company of Peter, James, and John, along with the appearance of Moses and Elijah. Jesus' transfiguration involves his face shining like the sun and his clothes turning dazzling white. A voice from the cloud says, "This is my Son, the Beloved; with him I am well pleased; listen to him!" (v. 5). Jesus later orders his disciples: "Tell no one about the vision until after the Son of Man has been raised from the dead" (v. 9).

In 2 Peter the disciples are reminded of being witnesses to Jesus' transfiguration and of his majesty and glory. They're encouraged to be attentive to the Holy Spirit speaking through them to action and to the world.

Transfiguration, transformation, and witnesses are themes of today's lessons. It often takes an unexpected occurrence—perhaps eyewitness contact that offers a new perspective—to transform a person into an advocate. In our modern times so much emphasis is placed on proof, but here we may be talking about an epiphany, an "Aha!" moment.

Share with the congregation some epiphany events in your life that changed you, opened your eyes and ears to circumstances of those different from you. Share an experience that changed your beliefs from the status quo.

Mountaintops aren't the only places from which new viewpoints can arise. Challenge your congregation to Lenten walks of justice in the areas of public transportation, a living wage, healthcare, childcare, or some other burning issue in your community. Perhaps you could do the Stations of the Cross, connecting this experience with a justice issue, offering time for reflection.

Sometimes just walking and learning can result in greater awareness, opening space for transformation and advocacy that can lead to changes in the system.

Public Transportation—If there is a bus system in your area, take the bus to work, to the grocery store, and to church to get a sense of what it's like and how inadequate it might be. Talk with persons who work for or with you to see how many buses they take and the time involved, including dropping a child off at daycare. At the end make recommendations and work with public transportation advocates for change.

Living Wage and Food Stamps—There's been a lot of controversy about living wage proposals in some localities. Try living on that wage for a week and you'll see that it's really not a lot. Live during Lent on a grocery budget based on the amount of food stamps that a family of your size earning the minimum wage would receive or on what senior citizens in your congregation get. At the end reflect on your learning and seek ways to be more responsive to those who are dependent on food stamps.

Healthcare—Do a congregational survey among seniors and others on the cost of their prescriptions, on the adequacy of their health insurance, and how much they have to pay. See if there are persons not covered by insurance and why. Evaluate the survey results for action. What can you as a congregation do? How can you lobby the government? How can you work with healthcare advocates in your community to make a difference?

Reflect again on how eye-opening, mountaintop experiences can truly change us when we return to life in the valleys.

Children's Time

Talk to the children about transformation. Share stories about moths and butterflies, and have them join in the story, since they will probably know it. Also talk about seeds becoming plants, fruit, and flowers and how the seed changes, is transfigured. Use this to segue into the Gospel and share the miraculous, astounding story. It would be interesting to have the children help to act out the Gospel. You may also want to talk about the ways our lives are transfigured, asking them how it felt when they began to read, to write, to talk, or to swim.

Musical Suggestions

Christ upon the mountain peak—EH 129, 130

O light of light—EH 133, 134

Songs of thankfulness and praise—EH 135

Jesu, Jesu—EH 602

Where cross the crowded ways of life—EH 609

Glen Bengson

Ash Wednesday

RCL: Joel 2:1-2, 12-17 or Isaiah 58:1-12; Psalm 51:1-17; 2 Corinthians
5:20b–6:10; Matthew 6:1-6, 16-21

LM: Joel 2:12-18; Psalm 51:3-4, 5-6ab, 12-13, 14, 17; 2 Corinthians
5:20–6:2; Matthew 6:1-6, 16-18

Lent recalls the foundation of our Christian discipleship, Jesus'
death and resurrection. That discipleship lives through faith in God
and serves the neighbor in Jesus' name. Lent historically has been a
time of preparation for baptism. We enter the community of Christian
faith and are daily renewed in faith through repentance, returning to
the love of God and of neighbor so that we can serve hungry people
and act justly in confidence and courage.

Throughout Lent sermons can focus on our ministry with and for
hungry people, on God's justice in the world, on connecting Jesus' life
of passionate commitment with our commitment to respond to human
needs today. This integrates the Sunday texts, the seasonal unity, and
the real life situations every congregation faces in its own community.

In my ministry for hungry people over the years, I have tried to
keep at least six action areas in mind: prayer, charitable financial giving,
volunteer participation, my own lifestyle habits, education, and advocacy. Each has its own importance and effect, and together they offer a
holistic approach to just action on behalf of hungry people. Worship
during Lent offers the context for these acts, equipping the congregation to go forth as disciples in the Lord's service to hungry and poor
people.

As Lent begins with Ash Wednesday, we're reminded of our mortality: "You are dust, and to dust you shall return." As the words are spoken, often the sign of the cross is marked on our forehead with ashes, recalling our baptism and inviting us into the Lenten discipline of repentance. I remember one baptism I performed involving a four-year-old girl. When I visited the family sometime later, I asked if the child had mentioned anything of the experience. "Oh, yes," said the mother, "she would point to her forehead and tell me that the pastor made a cross there. I said that you couldn't see it anymore, and she said, 'But God can.'" Building on these memories and experiences in worship, we help children (and adults) realize what it means to be a child of God and how in trusting God we reach out to our neighbors in love, justice, and peace.

In the Ash Wednesday Gospel from Matthew, Jesus speaks to his disciples about the traditional disciplines God's people embrace—charity, prayer, and fasting. He cautions them against self-promotion, obviously assuming that his followers will exercise these practices of piety in their own faith life. "When you give alms . . . when you pray . . . when you fast," he says, fix your focus on honoring God, not yourself. We shape our piety to respond to the needs of others.

Giving alms seems fairly self-evident. We share with those in need the material blessings God has given us. Is Lent a good time to have a special emphasis on your church's hunger appeal offering? Studies show that our denominational hunger programs are among the most effective ways to fund emergency relief, long-term development projects, and other efforts to help hungry people.

Surely we will undergird whatever we do with prayer—in worship, in our homes, and in personal devotional time. The section omitted from today's assigned text, Matthew 6:7-15, is about the Lord's Prayer. Sometimes what's left out of the text is the most important to emphasize. A Lenten study or sermon series on prayer, based on the petitions of the Lord's Prayer, could begin on Ash Wednesday. Such a series, with the petition "Give us this day our daily bread" as its heart, would complement an emphasis on hunger. Intercessory prayer is a form of advocacy. We advocate for others before God and offer ourselves as instruments of justice and peace for God's use.

If we focus on the tragedy of hunger, we can hardly forget the third discipline, fasting. Recent studies claim that 61 percent of United States citizens are overweight. But fasting in Scripture is about much more than controlling our poundage. It concerns our sense of dependence upon God to provide what we need. In Isaiah 58:1-12, "fasting" is an analogy to worship. Proper fasting, or worship, is acting justly toward others, freeing those in bondage, sharing bread with the hungry, and clothing the naked. When worship and action are complementary, God's people witness with integrity and God's intentions are fulfilled.

The last words of the Gospel text speak of establishing the proper "treasure." Here I'm reminded of St. Lawrence, a martyred deacon in the third century, during the persecution under Valerian. Summoned to the throne and told to bring all the treasures of the church with him, Lawrence appears, surrounded by lepers, orphans, people who are blind and lame. "Here are the treasures of the church," he says. In response, an outraged emperor has Lawrence killed. Where is our treasure, as individuals and as a Church? Will Lent, beginning with repentance on Ash Wednesday, help us identify once more what our heart treasures, where our confidence rests, and what disciplines of faith will help us live treasuring as God does?

Children's Time

If you have time with children in this service, consider teaching and distributing the following table blessings for use during Lent:

> Come, Lord Jesus, be our guest, and let these gifts to us be blest.
> Blessed be God, who is our Bread; may all the world be clothed and fed.
> —*Traditional Table Prayer*

> Gracious God, give bread to those who are hungry;
> And to us, who have bread, give the hunger for justice.

Musical Suggestions

Where Charity and Love Prevail—LBW 126

Praise and Thanksgiving—LBW 409

Son of God, Eternal Savior—LBW 364

Arise, Your Light has Come!—WOV 652

Jesu, Jesu, Fill Us With Your Love—WOV 765 (also BP 218)

Let Justice Flow Like Streams—WOV 763

All Praise to You for Honored Souls—BP 80

Creator God, Who Gives the Earth—BP 191

Glen Bengson

First Sunday of Lent

RCL: Genesis 2:15-17; 3:1-7; Psalm 32; Romans 5:12-19; Matthew 4:1-11

LM: Genesis 2:7-9; 3:1-7; Psalm 51:3-4, 5-6, 12-13, 17; Romans 5:12-19 or 5:12, 17-19; Matthew 4:1-11

This Sunday takes us to a garden and the wilderness to face temptation. Who are we, and will we live our true identity or succumb to the lure of other voices and claims on our life? Who is our God, and will we be faithful and live in accord with our professions of loyalty to God?

The reading from Genesis identifies the roots of sin in humankind's desire to "be like God" and to gain control of life for ourselves. We see creation's goodness and forget God's word that creation is for all to enjoy. We can see the results of our possessiveness all around us—in environmental degradation, material greed, and economic and political injustice.

Humankind's first task is to till the soil and care for creation (v. 15). Food is a necessity for human life, yet temptation also comes from eating. Food can be the occasion for great celebration and human community or the occasion for greed and human alienation.

Sin breaks relationships, with God and with our neighbors. God wants healing and reconciliation in our lives for us to experience life in its intended joy and abundance. Psalm 32 (or Psalm 51 in the Roman Catholic Lectionary) helps us voice our confession and rest our hopes on God's grace for new life.

"Umntu, Ngamntu, Ngabantu." This African phrase means "A person is not a person without other people." Concerns about justice for poor and hungry people are, at root, concerns for interrelationships of people with one another, with the environment, and with God. The Church is a place to image the kind of just and peaceful human relationships God intends for all people to share as we live together as God's children.

In Matthew's temptation story, Jesus, after his baptism, is "led by the Spirit" into the wilderness to face trials. So our baptism, when we enter the community of Christ and are gifted by the Spirit, sends us out into the wilderness of the world to grapple with life's temptations, the forces of evil, and the tests of faith that daily come our way.

Jesse Jackson's preaching litany "I am somebody" affirms people created in God's image. Satan seeks to exploit that identity in tempting Jesus. "IF you are the Son of God" could also be translated "SINCE you are . . ." When Satan, or demons in other passages, or those gathered at the cross who hurl insults at Jesus (Matthew 27) use these words of recognition, they tempt Jesus to deny who he is and misuse his identity and power for his own needs. We confront the same temptation. Will we betray our identities as God's children with selfish actions that aim to control life for our own benefit?

Jesus' first temptation is to "command these stones to become bread," a curious echo of God's first task to humans in Genesis, namely, to create nourishment by tilling the soil. Jesus responds, "One does not live by bread alone." One of my favorite cartoons has a character standing in front of a huge ice cream sundae saying exactly those words. Even Scripture can be quoted to fulfill our own desires rather than point us to living and acting for others so that all can have bread.

Remember that it is in a situation of extreme hunger, after forty days of fasting, that Jesus faces these tests. Would Jesus remain faithful to God's intentions and purpose? Each Christian faces the same challenge and opportunity daily.

In the Holy Land, the Mount of Temptation, where tradition says Jesus faced these trials, rises above the Palestinian town of Jericho. Our tour group stopped there for refreshment at the Temptation Restaurant, a rather large restaurant and souvenir shop. Ironies were apparent as we enjoyed plentiful food in a place associated with hunger, and were offered abundant wares to satisfy our materialistic impulses. Perhaps that's how the rest of the world sees our North American and European societies—overflowing with food and life's luxuries while others face hunger and even starvation daily. While we may fast voluntarily during Lent, many endure a daily fast they do not choose.

A further irony at the Mount of Temptation is the cable-car ride that whisks you to the summit, with views down on the kingdoms of the world. In Western societies it is very tempting to look down on others in our world, worshiping not God but the systems, people, and circumstances that give us such a privileged view. "Worship the Lord your God, and serve only him," Jesus says to Satan and to us.

Children's Time

Martin Luther explains the First Article of the Apostles' Creed: "I believe that God has created me and all that exists. God has given me and still preserves my body and soul. . . . In addition, God daily and abundantly provides food and drink, house and home . . . along with all the necessities of life. . . . God does all this out of pure, fatherly, and divine goodness and mercy, without any merit or worthiness of mine at all! For all of this I surely ought to thank and praise, serve and obey him."[1]

Invite the children forward and ask them what they're thankful for, what is most important to them. You'll get some of the above answers and others. These may be gifts of God for which we are thankful and that we seek to honor and use in the best way possible. Close with a prayer of thanks and commitment.

Musical Suggestions

A Mighty Fortress Is Our God—LBW 228, 229

Let Us Break Bread Together—LBW 212

O God of Earth and Altar—LBW 428

One Bread, One Body—WOV 710

Let Us Talents and Tongues Employ—WOV 754 (also BP 213)

Seek Ye First the Kingdom of God—WOV 783

Creator God, Who Gives the Earth—BP 191

1. *Luther's Small Catechism* (Minneapolis: Augsburg Fortress, 1994) 25.

Glen Bengson

Second Sunday of Lent

RCL: Genesis 12:1-4a; Psalm 121; Romans 4:1-5, 13-17; John 3:1-17
or Matthew 17:1-9

LM: Genesis 12:1-4a; Psalm 33:4-5, 18-19, 20, 22; 2 Timothy 1:8b-10;
Matthew 17:1-9

This Sunday's readings offer us "the Gospel in a nutshell," as one
description has characterized John 3:16: "God so loved the world."
God's concern is for the whole of creation and for all people.

This Sunday the prayer of the church should particularly relate to
the concerns for people around the globe, for hungry and oppressed
people, for refugees, and for the environment. If God is so in love with
creation, we should be too and show it in prayer that points to opportunities to express that love. The recent theory that there are only "six
degrees of separation" between me and any other person reminds us
that by God's creative grace we are connected to one another, blessed
by God's own Beloved One offered for our redemption.

The Gospel text contains the image, from the book of Numbers, of
the serpent held before the people of Israel so that they could be
healed. A serpent wrapped around a pole is the symbol for physicians,
gifted with the skills of healing. Perhaps this sign of healing, intended
for all who would look, reminds us that God intends healing for all
people. One current challenge to our faith and imaginations and commitment of resources is to ensure quality healthcare for all people. This
is inevitably a political as well as an economic question that calls us to
advocacy.

A doctor from Tanzania once visited our area for ten weeks, going from one congregation to another. He was astounded at our medical facilities, not to mention the general level of wealth in the United States. Visiting an emergency room with each patient area equipped with oxygen outlets in the wall, he told how his hospital, with 200 beds, had only two oxygen tanks, and one always had to be on ready in the surgery unit. He heard the litany "God bless America" and was puzzled. "God has already blessed you so much. Do you want more?"

The lesson from Genesis recounts God's call and promise to Abraham. As I write this reflection, the Middle East is in terrible turmoil again, as Israeli and Palestinian contend for the land of Abraham with great violence and increasing hatred. World history involves constant struggles to control land. The psalmist's affirmation "The earth is the Lord's and all that is in it" (Ps 24:1) ought to be the bottom line, but regretfully it is not. God's promise indeed connects blessing with land, but only in the broader intent that "in you all the families of the earth shall be blessed." The blessing is God's to give, for the sake of the recipient and all people, together residing on the land God gives and loves. We are to be the agents of that blessing, using God's land to produce blessing for all people, not simply the few, the privileged, the powerful. From that land can come abundance and life-giving food.

In one Lutheran Synod antihunger advocates came up with the idea to "Give an Abraham," meaning to contribute five dollars to the church's hunger appeal. This rings with the implications of giving so that others may be blessed and calls people beyond the pocket-change mentality of contributing. Since a different Abraham (Lincoln) is on that five-dollar bill, the appeal might evoke some of the heritage of Lincoln and his healing words for the nation in his second inaugural address, as the Civil War wound to its conclusion.

Moses finally viewed that "promised land" from the top of Mount Nebo, overlooking the Jordan Valley, the Dead Sea, and the mountains of eastern Israel. On a clear day you can't see forever, but you can make out Jerusalem, tucked away on the summits in the distance. At this overlook on Mount Nebo a sculpture has been raised—a serpent entwined into a cross. This reminder of the healing serpent of the wilderness, and for Christians the healing power of the cross of Christ, casts a shadow of hope and promise over a land so beset by trouble. There is conflict, animosity, hunger, sickness, and a host of other ills arising out of both nature's geography and fickle weather patterns and humankind's sinful assertions. Yet God's promise is that there will be blessing for all the families of the world God loves. There will be healing and salvation, because the Son is lifted up in sacrifice and triumph. Eternity and the world and each of our lives are still in God's hands.

(Roman Catholic Lectionary readings for the Second Sunday of Lent are traditionally of the Transfiguration, this year from Matthew 17:1-9. See Transfiguration Sunday for this year, pp. 54–56).

Children's Time

John 3:16 is so well known that some good, concrete, visual, sensory experiences would help. "He's Got the Whole World in His Hands" is a song easily sung by every age, with room for a great creativity (perhaps finding some less gender-specific language) and flexibility in verses that can express what is on the hearts and minds of the local community in facing the issues of their moment. I've used a blown-up beach ball on which the world is imprinted, passing it around as we sing, giving everyone a sense that they are God's steward, with the world literally in their hands. Another option is to have people hold the globe and offer a prayer. Children, especially, can relate to these activities, and it is good way to do a "children's message" that involves everybody.

Musical Suggestions

The Church of Christ, in Every Age—LBW 433

God, Who Stretched the Spangled Heavens—LBW 463

Take My Life, that I May Be—LBW 406

O God of Mercy, God of Light—LBW 425

Christ is Alive! Let Christians Sing—LBW 363

Listen, God is Calling—WOV 712

The Spirit Sends Us Forth to Serve—WOV 723

Blest are They—WOV 764

Go, My Children, with My Blessing—WOV 721

Creator God, Who Gives the Earth—BP 191

Hope of the World—BP 176

God of the Universe—BP 162

Glen Bengson

Third Sunday of Lent

RCL: Exodus 17:1-7; Psalm 95; Romans 5:1-11; John 4:5-42
LM: Exodus 17:3-7; Psalm 95:1-2, 6-7, 8-9; Romans 5:1-2, 5-8;
John 4:5-42 or 4:5-15, 19b-26, 39a, 40-42

Today's reading from the book of Exodus takes us back into the wilderness with Israel, as they complain about their difficult conditions and wonder if they were better off under bondage in Egypt. What a contrast to their earlier cries for deliverance! Is this reminiscent of our own culture, in which every improvement in living conditions apparently leaves people no happier than before? How quickly they forget, we often say, of our selective memory. Didn't Israel remember their cry to God (Exod 2:23-25), which God heard and to which God responded through Moses, leading Israel out of Egypt?

I once heard Jack Nelson-Pallmeyer tell of visiting Calcutta and his angry reaction to the abysmal poverty and hunger he saw in that city of millions. "I wanted to scream at God and shout, 'How can you tolerate such suffering?' And then it hit me. In the suffering of the poor, God was shouting at me, and for that matter, at all of us and our social systems that cause and perpetuate hunger, poverty, and inequality." If we listen at all, we can still hear the cries of the people, the cry of God.

In the Exodus text, the people "thirsted for water." In John's Gospel Jesus meets a woman at the well. She is intrigued by his offer of "living water" and the prospect of never again being thirsty. People around the world long for that reality, and not only in a spiritual sense. Church World Service/CROP Walks have an ongoing theme, "We walk, because they walk." This links the ten-kilometer length of the CROP Walk to the laborious, daily walk that many people around the world take to bring home fresh water for that day's needs for cooking, drinking, and washing.

Many denominational relief and development agencies provide resources to dig wells to provide fresh water, develop ponds for local fish-raising industries, clean up polluted water, or teach sustainable agricultural methods that conserve and make the best use of local natural resources. In such ways "living water" can became a reality for more people and enhance their lives.

The Samaritan at the well is a person of another culture and religion, a foreigner, a stranger. She is a woman. All these identities presented problems in Jesus' world, and still do in ours. Our nation struggles to welcome immigrants, who often come with few resources except their exceptional determination and innate skills and who meet suspicion and prejudice simply because they are different. They often suffer "guilt by association" because of what others do. Jesus offers the "living water" of hope to all people, of deliverance from the oppressive practices that deny people their true dignity, and the assurance that God does not judge on the basis of society's values but "in spirit and in truth."

After experiencing the "living water" of God's "amazing grace," the woman cannot help but share the good news, running to tell others. Bread for the World members tell the good news of God's care for poor and hungry people, inviting others who thirst for hope to be part of a vibrant ministry. Bread for the World members contact their members of Congress, write letters to the editor of their local newspapers, and use Bread for the World Sunday resources to encourage others to become advocates for hungry people. Church denominational gatherings, clergy association meetings, ecumenical conferences, and community group events become opportunities for personal testimony to the work of Bread for the World.

The Samaritan woman does not know how people will respond, but she has a passion to tell about the good news in her life—and others respond. God promises that "my word . . . shall not return to me empty, but it shall accomplish that which I purpose" (Isa 55:11). Advocates for poor and hungry people speak with the confidence that comes from knowing they give voice to the concerns of people for whom God cares deeply. U.S. senator Paul Simon often said that in his experience "one letter to a member of Congress on a hunger issue saves a life."[1] Our personal testimony for those who hunger will not return empty.

Children's Time

One of the great photographs from the 1930s Depression is of a woman, her face lined with sadness, weariness, worry; head resting in one hand; holding one baby while two young children hide their faces behind each of her shoulders; clothes rough, worn, dirty. She is the very picture of a person at the edge of her world, wondering if tomorrow simply holds more of the same, trying to exist day to day. Her image sparked a national reaction to provide aid to migrant workers, but she never benefited at the time, continuing to move from place to place.

Just recently her story was told in the *Smithsonian* magazine (March 2002). In 1975 the photographer located her and interviewed her and her three daughters, now grown with their own families. She was a migrant worker in a "pea-pickers camp," 32 years old, though she looked much older. She and her daughters had been living on frozen vegetables and birds the children had killed. She had just sold the tires on her car to buy food. They lived, with only a quilt to cover them, under the very bridges John Steinbeck had described in *The Grapes of Wrath*. Somehow they had survived.

How many migrant workers, and others, still languish in such conditions today? How can the Church serve as their voice, advocating for just working conditions, medical attention, and educational opportunities for their children? Find this photo, available as a poster, and simply ask the children what they see, what they feel, when they look at the woman's picture. Is this how those without food, without home, without hope might look? If you felt like this, what could people do to help you? What can we do to help feed them, house them, offer them work that pays, give them hope? Adults will want to see it, too, and perhaps talk about these things.

---

1. Quoted in Arthur Simon, *Christian Faith and Public Policy: No Grounds for Divorce* (Grand Rapids, Mich.: William B. Eerdmans Publishing Company, 1987) 106.

Musical Suggestions

Son of God, Eternal Savior—LBW 364

Where Cross the Crowded Ways of Life—LBW 429 (also BP 174)

In Christ There Is No East or West—LBW 359 (also BP 87)

When Israel Was in Egypt's Land—WOV 670

For All the Faithful Women—WOV 692

You Satisfy the Hungry Heart (Gift of Finest Wheat)—WOV 711

Here in This Place (Gather Us In)—WOV 718

My Soul Proclaims Your Greatness—WOV 730

I, the Lord of Sea and Sky (Here I Am, Lord)—WOV 752
   (also BP 129)

Let Justice Flow like Streams—WOV 763

Banquet of Praise in Justice Spread—BP 79

God of Justice, God of Mercy—BP 86

I've Got Peace Like a River—BP 113

Brothers and Sisters of Mine Are the Hungry—BP 148

Help, O Lord, the Thrown Away—BP 150

Glen Bengson

Fourth Sunday of Lent

RCL: 1 Samuel 16:1-13; Psalm 23; Ephesians 5:8-14; John 9:1-41
LM: 1 Samuel 16:1b, 6-7, 10-13a; Psalm 23:1-3a, 3b-4, 5, 6;
    Ephesians 5:8-14; John 9:1-41 or 9:1, 6-9, 13-17, 34-38

The passage from 1 Samuel tells of Samuel anointing David as the king of Israel, succeeding Saul. Anointing with oil evokes rich images from the Scriptures and in Christian faith. Anointing is a way to officially recognize a person's authority as king, priest, or prophet. It is a sign of God's healing power and is part of the historic baptismal rite, a sign of the Spirit working in the newly baptized person. Jesus is the Christ, the Messiah, literally "the anointed one." As Christ is acknowledged as "King," healing is brought to those in distress, people are welcomed into the fellowship of the church, and the justice of God is prophetically proclaimed.

Psalm 23 continues the theme: "The Lord is my shepherd . . . he anoints my head with oil." Images of being chosen, of healing, and of hospitality come to mind. When the psalmist continues, "You prepare a table before me, in the presence of my enemies," we see a God who provides under the most difficult circumstances, who desires that enemies be reconciled and strangers welcomed. The Middle Eastern custom of hospitality, shared by many cultures, is to welcome all visitors and to break bread with both friend and stranger. Jesus' ministry centers on table fellowship with outcasts, sinners, and those rejected by others. His ministry images the kingdom of God, when

71

friends and enemies are gathered into one at the great banquet of eternity, reconciled and at peace. Is this what our church communion celebrations, our family meals, our potluck suppers, and our national and international food policies proclaim?

Many churches host meals during the week; all are invited. Our church hosts "The Caring Place," a ministry of all the churches in our small Ohio town. Each Thursday evening a different church prepares a meal, brings it to the church and, with other volunteers, serves the guests. The guests don't have to go through a line but are served at their table. They can have as much as they want. There is good talk and fellowship, and children have a special place. It is one way that we believe the Good Shepherd "prepares a table" for those he has anointed with his love and with whom he desires to share in the heavenly banquet. How can it be extended to embrace the whole world of God's creating and loving care? Perhaps through our denominational hunger relief and development programs, through evangelism outreach in our local communities, and through prophetic words to our governmental leaders, advocating governance that images that of the Anointed One, caring for all his flock, leading them to green pastures, by still waters, and to the table of the kingdom.

John's Gospel tells the story of the man born blind, whom Jesus heals and whose situation provokes a great discussion about sin and salvation. The authorities want to blame the victim and his family: "Rabbi, who sinned, this man or his parents, that he was born blind?" (v. 2). How reminiscent of our own day, as those in poverty, hungry and homeless people, and others in need of healing in their lives are denied help or receive the most limited assistance because others blame them for conditions beyond their control. While all people certainly have a measure of personal responsibility in any situation, we know, as did Jesus, that there are structural and natural forces at work that call for a societal response. Jesus rejects the "blame game," instead declaring that human needs become the opportunity to reveal God's work of mercy and healing. Jesus identifies himself as the one who comes to bear witness to that mercy, to be "the light of the world" in this case.

The story is told of the wise teacher who asks his students, "How can one tell when night has given way to the day?" The students propose answers focused on discerning the physical evidence of light versus darkness, trying to define what constitutes "dawn," but none of the answers receive the teacher's approval. Finally they ask their teacher for the correct answer. "Night becomes day," he says, "when you see in the face of the stranger your brother or sister." The light of Christ reveals that we are all one in the grace of God and related to one another, not out of our own choosing, but by being created in God's image and redeemed in Christ.

Children's Time

Today's pericope from Ephesians evokes the images of darkness and light. One song that everyone can sing is "This Little Light of Mine," encouraging us to "let it shine" in witness to the Light of the World. Younger children enjoy singing this with the accompanying hand motions and could lead the whole congregation in remembering their vocation as enlightened children of God. The experience is the message. It could be complemented by all holding candles, gathering around the baptismal font, or in procession. A verse connected to baptism is "Let your light shine before others, so that they may see your good works and give glory to your Father in heaven" (Matt 5:16). It might even make an effective closing to worship, signifying the church going out into the world bearing the light of Christ. How can we bring the light of Christ to others? By recognizing that it is Christ's light and Christ's healing that we have received and can now share.

Musical Suggestions

God, Whose Almighty Word (Let there be light!)—LBW 400

The King of Love My Shepherd Is—LBW 456

Amazing Grace, How Sweet the Sound—LBW 448 (also BP 105)

I Want to Walk as a Child of the Light—WOV 649

We are Marching in the Light of God (Siyahamba)—WOV 650

Shine, Jesus, Shine—WOV 651

Word of God, Come Down on Earth—WOV 716

Healer of Our Every Ill—WOV 738

Be Thou My Vision—WOV 776 (also BP 99)

Lord Jesus, If I Love and Serve My Neighbor—BP 95

The Lord Hears the Cry of the Poor—BP 109

All Who Love and Serve Your City—BP 165

Glen Bengson

Fifth Sunday of Lent

RCL: Ezekiel 37:1-14; Psalm 130; Romans 8:6-11; John 11:1-45

LM: Ezekiel 37:12-14; Psalm 130:1-2, 3-4, 5-6, 7-8; Romans 8:8-11;
  John 11:1-45 or 11:3-7, 17, 20-27, 33b-45

This week brings us to the tomb of Lazarus, as Jesus responds to his friends' pleas and Martha's and Mary's faith. Jesus calls Lazarus forth from the tomb, a preview of things to come, a threat to those who think they hold the power of life and death, and evidence that God is the one who has the last word. Such a rich story will have many layers of meaning for us today, as it has always had for the Church.

The Lutheran Order for Confession begins, "Most merciful God, we confess that we are in bondage to sin, and cannot free ourselves." We could just as well say, "in bondage to sin and death," because they are so intimately connected. But the good news is that the bondage is broken by Jesus' power. Jesus directs the dead man's friends, "Unbind him, and let him go" (v. 44). He speaks the same words to us. In Christ, through his death and resurrection, the powers of death are broken, and we are free to live a new life, to offer our lives in service for the sake of Jesus. "Unbind us and let us go" could be the words of Moses to Pharaoh, declaring that the children of God should not be in bondage to any exploitative earthly rule. "Unbind them and let them go" can be the words of advocates of life speaking to the principalities and powers that hold others in the bondage of hunger, homelessness, hopelessness, and oppression.

Sometimes those forces of bondage even work through the façade of religion. I remember a visit to Haiti with the Lutheran Hunger Program. One of our Haitian guides remarked that in Port-au-Prince there were as many storefront churches as there were bars. Both do the same thing, he said: they give people an escape from the reality of their oppression. Jesus does not offer an escape from sin and death, but victory over them. Jesus does not avoid them, but confronts them head on. Death makes him weep in sorrow for the grief and pain and loss it causes. But he does not shrink from the smell of death and calls Lazarus forth into the fresh air of God's presence and power. In Christ we have been freed from the power of death that makes us think only of ourselves to a life we can freely offer for the sake of others. Instead of simply seeking to preserve our own life, we see in Christ the power of life offered up in the service of God.

God's Spirit is the power for such life. The passage from Ezekiel is the familiar vision of the valley of dry bones. God's breath moving over the barren bones rejuvenates them, once more raising them to link and live. It is a parable of God's gracious gift of new life to God's people Israel—and for Christians, to the Church. A powerful example of that Spirit bringing life and hope out of the desert of death was the Jubilee 2000 gathering in Washington in June of 2000. Hundreds were able to gather in support of debt relief for the poorest nations, and therefore the poorest people, of the world. Linking hands, we circled the U.S. Treasury building in a sign of solidarity. It was an invitation to the world's leaders to use their power to help poor nations needing financial resources to feed their hungry, house their homeless, heal their sick, educate their children, and develop their human potential toward self-sufficiency. The Spirit was present, breathing life and hope where only death seemed to be present. How and where can we continue to link with others and let the Spirit rattle the dry bones back to life?

Children's Time

Think about going outside on a cold morning and blowing your breath, your air, into the cooler air. You can see your breath! That's like the Church. God blows his Spirit into the Church, and the actions of the Church become the sign of that breath of God. We all know we can't stay under water for very long. We need to come up to breathe.

Just as we need air to live, we need the Spirit of God to live our Christian lives. That's one reason it's important for us to be in church and to gather with other Christians as we do today, so that we can share the Spirit, the breath of God, the love of God, with one another and with the world.

Musical Suggestions

Peace, to Soothe Our Bitter Woes—LBW 338

Rise Up, O Saints of God!—LBW 383 (also BP 126)

Before You, Lord, We Bow—LBW 401

O Holy Spirit, Enter In—LBW 459

Holy Spirit, Ever Dwelling—LBW 523

The Spirit Sends Us Forth to Serve—WOV 723

Lord, You Give the Great Commission—WOV 756 (also BP 106)

I Am the Bread of Life—WOV 702 (also BP 124)

Spirit, Spirit of Gentleness—WOV 684

Baptized in Water—WOV 693

We Were Baptized in Christ Jesus—WOV 698

Breathe on Me, Breath of God—BP 88

Spirit of the Living God—BP 102/103

Lord, Make Us Servants of Your Peace—BP 157

Glen Bengson

Passion Sunday/Palm Sunday

Liturgy of the Palms

RCL: Matthew 21:1-11; Psalm 118:1-2, 19-29

LM: Matthew 21:1-11

Liturgy of the Passion

RCL: Isaiah 50:4-9a; Psalm 31:9-16; Philippians 2:5-11; Matthew
   26:14–27:66 or Matthew 27:11-54

LM: Isaiah 50:4-7; Psalm 22:8-9, 17-18, 19-20, 23-24; Philippians 2:6-11;
   Matthew 26:14–27:66 or 27:11-54

Passion or Palm Sunday marks the beginning of Holy Week, the heart and center of the Christian year.

The processional Gospel, Mathew 21:1-11, is an unmistakable political scene. The people long for deliverance from their Roman oppressors and their accomplices. They acclaim Jesus as "Son of David," the Messiah they hope will finally bring that salvation. He is that king, but not in the way they expect and desire. God's rule in the world is going to be different, exercising not brute force and coercion, but the power of love, forgiveness, and hope. It does not shy away from calling sin what it is and calling the powers of the world to account. Witness the lives of Rev. Martin Luther King, Jr. (killed on April 4) and Bishop Oscar Romero (March 24). But it does so with humility and love for the oppressors and perpetrators of evil, even while standing solidly with their victims. That is the power loosed by a King, a Romero, a Gandhi, and others. Jesus and his followers come to initiate the reign of peace and justice through the offering of their own lives. Perhaps it's a good Sunday to focus some attention on the Sunday offering in its true and full meaning, expressed in one way in the Lutheran liturgy: "Merciful Father, we offer with joy and thanksgiving what you have first given us—our selves, our time, and our possessions, signs of your gracious love" (LBW, p. 87).

The reading from chapters 26 and 27 of Matthew's Gospel begins with Jesus and his disciples at the Last Supper. Jesus' words are evocative of an earlier meal, the so-called feeding of the five thousand (plus many more women and children). The important point in each meal is that Jesus takes bread, blesses it, breaks it, and gives it to the disciples to eat and distribute. What seems like an insignificant, hopeless amount, placed in Jesus' hands, proves more than enough for all. In our communion celebrations we usually receive a small wafer, or a little piece of bread, a small sip of wine or grape juice, and this is called a "supper." But it is a foretaste of the feast to come, because it is given in remembrance of Jesus, recalling all that his life meant and means for us. It points us to the possibility of sharing what we have, not holding it close to save it for ourselves, but letting Jesus bless it for the sake of feeding all.

The Jewish Passover contains a litany to which the response is "dayenu!," which means "it would have been enough." ("Had God brought us out of Egypt and not divided the sea for us, dayenu!" "Had God brought us to Mount Sinai and not given us the Torah, dayenu!") We trust that God will provide what we need, what is enough for life. How do we communicate and live God's promises so that others may come to trust in God's "dayenu!" and in fact experience what is "dayenu" for their lives? The Holy Communion strengthens and empowers God's people to "Go in peace, serve the Lord!" in the world.

The lesson from Philippians reminds us that Jesus did not seek equality with God but emptied and humbled himself. This, Paul says, is the mind to have: the mind, the heart, the self-giving in the image of Christ. I use this passage as a "last word," just prior to the benediction, to provide biblical commentary and explanation as we hear the Passion of the Lord read, hear Jesus despair for God's presence (see Psalm 22, the responsorial psalm in the Roman Catholic Lectionary), and give himself to death for our sake. The closing words of the text then point us to a week hence, when "Alleluias!" once more pour from our hearts and out of our mouths: "Therefore God has highly exalted him . . ."

The day began with a scene of political expectation and ends with Jesus crucified and buried. Hope seems to have been killed along with Jesus. In the movie *On the Waterfront,* Karl Malden plays the local priest, trying to serve a parish of dock workers facing corruption in their leadership. A falling pallet in the ship's hold kills a fellow worker, a deed the mob has ordered. Malden comes to give the victim the last rites, then starts to leave. He stops and looks toward the gathered onlookers, workers, and mob power brokers. He speaks of Christ's crucifixion having happened once more and of Jesus' presence right there with them at that very moment. The church, he says, is not off in some building but right there in that hold, where death has seemed to reign. He tells them that they are the ones who can put a stop to such abuse of power, destruction of lives, and denial of justice. "Let the same mind be in you that was in Christ Jesus," he seems to be saying, echoing St. Paul.

Children's Time

Since children of all ages like parades, a good way to get the younger members of the congregation on board at the beginning of worship is to involve them in a procession. They could start from an area outside the sanctuary and come into the church worship area, leading the rest of the congregation with their "Hosannas" and maybe a simple song. They should have palm branches and perhaps colored robes and other light clothing to wave. Ask them questions about where Jesus is going and what it means to follow Jesus. This would spark their attention to the rest of the service and the lengthy reading of the Passion (which could be done as a liturgical reading involving members taking the part of the characters in the drama).

Musical Suggestions

God of Grace and God of Glory—LBW 415

Lead On, O King Eternal!—LBW 495

Lord, Whose Love in Humble Service—LBW 423

Lord of Glory, You Have Bought Us—LBW 424

For the Bread Which You Have Broken—LBW 200

Jesu, Jesu, Fill Us with Your Love—WOV 765 (also BP 218)

A New Commandment—WOV 664

Bind Us Together—WOV 748

Let Us Talents and Tongues Employ—WOV 754 (also BP 213)

Bread of the World in Mercy Broken—BP 110

Lord of All Nations, Grant Me Grace—BP 178

James Dunn

Holy (Maundy) Thursday

RCL: Exodus 12:1-4 (5-10), 11-14; Psalm 116:1-2, 12-19;
1 Corinthians 11:23-26; John 13:1-17, 31b-35
LM: Exodus 12:1-8, 11-14; Psalm 116:12-13, 15-16bc, 17-18;
1 Corinthians 11:23-26; John 13:1-15

Mark Hatfield, a United States senator from Oregon for many years, wrote in 1976: "There has been a tragic and unbiblical separation between witnessing to the good news of Christ and acting with his love to meet human need. How dare we present the Christ as the bread of life to a hungry man and only be concerned with Christ as the spiritual bread, and not obey Christ by providing the physical bread to meet that man's physical needs of today?"[1] Yet today, Holy Thursday of all days, we should remember the inexorable link between food for the body and food for the soul. The Passover event in Exodus focused on food.

The reading from 1 Corinthians describes that on the night of his betrayal, Jesus took bread and initiated a meal with meaning that is the focal point for worship until this day. Eating and remembering, drinking and reflecting, communing at table and worshiping—these survival techniques have always gone together. Indeed, it is "a tragic and unbiblical separation" when we try to divide the Bread of Life from bread for life. Work and worship, food and faith, eating and learning,

1. James M. Dunn, Ben E. Loring, and Phil Strickland, *Endangered Species* (Nashville: Broadman Press, 1976) 3.

togetherness at the table and oneness in spirit have been part of a common experience since Jesus, as John's Gospel describes, washed his disciples' feet during supper.

Part of this binding, bonding, building experience is essential because it is so regular and oft-repeated. Christ chooses to make breaking bread and eating a common meal the venue for self-revelation. He was and is bread. He was and is living water. Christ has not changed. He showed himself to his disciples and he reveals himself to us as the bread and water that sustain his people. His presence is constant. He is in the ordinary events of life. The Wesley brothers wrote and spoke of the "ordinaries" of life. Jesus the Christ comes as the extraordinary God to ordinary people in daily life.

But everyone is invited to his banquet table, and that is the pattern for all of us who claim to be disciples. More than that, it is our explicit instruction: "If you know these things, blessed are you if you do them" (John 13:17). We are really getting down to the daily business of Christian living when we extend the Lord's Supper to all God's children. Bread is that which, if we have it, we take it for granted; but if we don't have it, nothing else is important to us until we get it. The world's cry is the cry for bread.

"In the whole process of continuing creation," Francis DuBose says, "God has brought the human family into partnership. The command to 'rule' nature is a commission to 'manage' the environment in such a way as to develop the God-given resources for the good of all."[2]

If we are irresponsible managers, evil CEOs, God's plan, God's work, is distorted, perverted, and ditched. Some enjoy (and suffer) excesses while others go hungry. Even a mother's milk for her babies will not come if she is undernourished. The problem of world hunger can only be solved as we return to the basic stewardship principle that God established when the world was made. Hungers, physical and spiritual, must be met together.

Children's Time [LH]

Ask the children how many of them like bread. If your service includes the Eucharist, gather the children around the table and talk

---

2. Gary Gunderson, ed., *Roots of Hope* (Decatur, Ga.: Oakhurst Baptist Church, 1979) 33.

about how bread is both ordinary and special. When we're eating dinner at home, someone may pass the bread and it becomes a part of our meal—usually not the central part, but something that goes along with everything else we eat. But for those in our world who have little to eat, bread can be key to life itself. And when we take part in communion in church, bread is at the central place because it has a different meaning, a meaning that took shape at a meal Jesus shared with his disciples before his death. It is that event we remember each time the Lord's Supper takes place in worship, but is especially in our minds and hearts on Holy Thursday. Invite the children to remember those special roles bread plays, for hungry people and for us as Jesus' followers, whenever we celebrate the Eucharist.

Musical Suggestions [LH]

Let Us Be Bread—GC 816

Bread for the World—GC 827

I Am the Bread of Life—BP 124

As We Gather at Your Table—FWS 2268

James Dunn

Good Friday

RCL: Isaiah 52:13–53:12; Psalm 22; Hebrews 10:16-25 or 4:14-16; 5:7-9; John 18:1–19:42

LM: Isaiah 52:13–53:12; Psalm 31:2, 6, 12-13, 15-16, 17, 25; Hebrews 4:14-16; 5:7-9; John 18:1–19:42

Jesus' crucifixion has continuing meaning for Christ's followers. It was a historical event on an actual hill at a specific point in time. Yet Christians see the cross's abiding relevance. The way to God, as always, involves accepting the redemptive work done on the cross.

The cross has a place in a practical theology for facing problems like world hunger. It is the unifying symbol of a distinctly Christian life. The cross reveals fully God's love for people and God's hatred for sin. We could never have known either of those if Christ had not died on the cross. Cross-bearers do not make lame excuses about their lack of compassion for haunting, hungry persons. The very cross in which Christ's followers claim redemption is the seal of God's love for all people, even those with bloated bellies and bony faces. Those who kneel at the cross have no difficulty mustering and sustaining indignation and anger at the power of corporate evil. They have seen evil at its worst. The very selfishness and greed that killed Christ is at work in the world still killing innocents (Isa 53:3).

The cross-life means that those who follow Jesus will, like him, seek not their own will but God's (John 20:21). It means giving of self and sacrificing privilege. It means changing society by the power of love and self-denial, putting others first and voluntarily surrendering self with redemptive purpose. The cross's meaning for contemporary life has been terribly narrowed, distorted, and perverted by those who see it only as the symbol of personal salvation. The cross makes us care about one another and ends hostility (Eph 2:16). The cross is central in a Christian social strategy. It involves returning good for evil, the strong serving the weak, the privileged working out problems with the underprivileged, the just taking upon themselves the sins of the unjust.

The New Testament doctrine of the resurrection has something to do with a theology for facing world hunger. The Christian belief that Jesus Christ actually did rise from the grave and literally conquer death is a source of real hope. This belief is far more than simply a personal promise of immortality. For believers, there is a different look toward the future than that of those who do not have the promise of the resurrection.

God is in history and is not through with humankind. God is still in control. Our efforts for positive change are never wasted. So when we passively resign ourselves to the evils of the day, we are sinful. The one who knows how to do good and does not do it is guilty of real sin (Jas 4:17).

It's hard to muster sufficient motivation to make the needed changes for the world to avoid starvation and ecological calamity. But Christians have a responsibility for the future. In a chapter entitled "What Has Posterity Ever Done for Me?" Robert L. Heilbroner puts it well:

> Will Mankind survive? Who knows? The question I want to put is more searching: Who cares? It is clear that most of us today do not care—or at least do not care enough. How many of us would be willing to give up some minor convenience—say, the use of aerosols—in the hope that this might extend the life of man on earth by a hundred years? Suppose we also know with a high degree of certainty that humankind could not survive a thousand years unless we gave up our wasteful diet of meat, abandoned all pleasure driving, cut back on every use of energy that was not essential. Would we care enough for posterity to pay the price of

its survival? . . . Even a century far exceeds our powers of empathetic imagination.[1]

Believers in Jesus Christ have the quality of hope for the future that permits—no, demands—that they work to identify with those yet unborn. Christians have a theology of hope. God is not trapped in history, a thing of the past, or up there somewhere out of touch with reality. Neither is the living God simply within us, confined by our apathy.

God is, rather, leading us, going on before us as with the children of Israel in the Exodus, as with Jesus in facing death. God is in and behind and under and above all the events of the week ahead, the years ahead, waiting for us to catch up (Psalm 22). A genuinely Christian eschatology is not so concerned with signs of the end times as with having the blessed hope in Jesus Christ. Precisely that ingredient, hope, is the one thing most necessary in tackling world hunger.

Children's Time [LH]

It's hard on a day when we come to grips with our Savior's death to talk to children honestly about things that may be on their minds. Many Good Friday services probably don't include a children's time, because the laughter and good spirits that often accompany these moments in worship are not the aura we want on Good Friday. But if there are moments with children, remind them of Heilbroner's point that it matters for us, in every time of life, to care about our children and their futures. Even on the cross, Jesus spoke to those he loved gathered around him about what they would do and how they would care for each other after he was gone (John 19:25-27). Even on days like this, we remember the needs of hungry people.

Musical Suggestions [LH]

Christ Is the Truth, the Way—BP 179

I Bind My Heart—GC 668

When I Survey the Wondrous Cross—UMH 298

O God, My God—NCH 515

1. Robert L. Heilbroner, *An Inquiry into the Human Prospect* (New York: W. W. Norton and Company, 1975) 169.

James Dunn

Easter Vigil

RCL: Genesis 1:1–2:4a; Psalm 136:1-9, 23-26; Genesis 7:1-5, 11-18; 8:6-18; 9:8-13; Psalm 46; Genesis 22:1-18; Psalm 16; Exodus 14:10-31; 15:20-21; Exodus 15:1b-13, 17-18; Isaiah 55:1-11; Isaiah 12:2-6; Proverbs 8:1-8, 19-21; 9:4b-6; Psalm 19; Ezekiel 36:24-28; Psalm 42 and 43; Ezekiel 37:1-14; Psalm 143; Zephaniah 3:14-20; Psalm 98; Romans 6:3-11; Psalm 114; Matthew 28:1-10

LM: Genesis 1:1–2:2 or 1:1, 26-31a; Psalm 104:1-2, 5-6, 10, 12, 13-14, 24, 35 or Psalm 33:4-5, 6-7, 12-13, 20-22; Genesis 22:1-18 or 22:1-2, 9a, 10-13, 15-18; Psalm 16:5, 8, 9-10, 11; Exodus 14:15–15:1; Exodus 15:1-2, 3-4, 5-6, 17-18; Isaiah 54:5-14; Psalm 30:2, 4, 5-6, 11-12, 13; Isaiah 55:1-11; Isaiah 12:2-3, 4, 5-6; Baruch 3:9-15, 32–4:4; Psalm 19:8, 9, 10, 11; Ezekiel 36:16-17a, 18-28; Psalm 42:3, 5; 43:3, 4 *(when baptism is celebrated);* Isaiah 12:2-3, 4bcd, 5-6 or Psalm 51:12-13, 14-15, 18-19 *(when baptism is not celebrated);* Romans 6:3-11; Psalm 118:1-2, 16-17, 22-23; Matthew 28:1-10

"I am constantly endeavoring to reduce my needs to the minimum. I feel morally guilty in ordering a costly meal for it deprives someone else of a slice of bread, some child, perhaps of a bottle of milk."[1] We squirm hearing these words of violinist Fritz Kreisler. The discomfort disappears quickly, however. We all now know that we're not supposed to feel guilty.

1. *Baptist Review* (Nov.–Dec. 1969) cover.

Yet it is timely on this dark day to remember the creation story in which the divine intent to perpetually provide for all humankind is clear (Gen 1:11-12, 29), and God's satisfaction with that scheme is declared "very good" (Gen 1:31).

If that were not enough for us to see the heavenly purpose, the biblical record is replete with reminders of God's steadfast love (*ḥesed*) which abides forever (Psalm 136). The message is clear and colorful: "Ho, everyone who thirsts, come to the waters; and you who have no money, come, buy and eat!" (Isa 55:1).

Indeed, God's promised and realized provision, God's steadfast love and calls to obey his voice (Gen 22:18) put us in perpetual debt to the Divine. Again, in this season we are reminded of the words of Jesus when he said, "From everyone to whom much has been given, much will be required" (Luke 12:48). There is such a thing as "good guilt," God-given guilt.

Awful oughtness is out these days. Duty is dead. In our era we have trouble identifying with Fritz Kreisler's motivation for simple living. Responsibility and requirement are not popular words. But face grace. Is guilt the issue after all? Luke 12:48 sets out the inexorable law of stewardship. If we observe this somber season with an orgy of apathy, we should feel guilty. If we celebrate God's great gift without caring and giving, we are violating one of Heaven's first principles.

We give food to hungry people, extend grace, share God's Word out of grateful hearts for the grace extended to us. The very act of giving shows that we have plugged into God's steadfast love, that we are aware of divine blessing.

As the rain falls on the just and the unjust and all humankind looks heavenward, so prayers and praise are offered up. The cycle of grace and gratitude is as real, as universal, and as dynamic as the physical cycle in which the waters come down, sustain the earth, and then evaporate, return, and repeat the process.

The one who receives much will, of course, give much. That is elemental justice, common fairness. Failing to respond to such a formula denies our humanity, the way in which we are all made in the image of God. Godliness alone can carry us across the dark day of sin at its worst and love at its best. Godliness, not guilt, marks our acceptance of moral responsibility for hungry and poor people and represents harmony with the divine order of things.

Children's Time [LH]

In many ways the Easter Vigil is a time of very expectant waiting, when we hear the stories of faith recounted anew. Children are used to that expectancy at Christmas, but Easter traditions are probably more varied. As we await Christ's fresh in-breaking as resurrected Lord in our lives, it may be hard to focus on the "oughts" that James Dunn discusses above. But what does Christ bring other than new life to all people, and isn't abundant food a part of the new life he promises? So with the expectancy comes a sense of commitment to the fullness of life for all and new resolve for us to play a role in ensuring that all are fed.

Musical Suggestions [LH]

Alleluia, Alleluia—UMH 162

Because You Live, O Christ—NCH 231

Come, You Faithful, Raise the Strain—NCH 230

James Dunn

Easter Sunday

RCL: Acts 10:34-43 or Jeremiah 31:1-6; Psalm 118:1-2, 14-24;
  Colossians 3:1-4 or Acts 10:34-43; John 20:1-18 or Matthew 28:1-10
LM: Acts 10:34a, 37-43; Psalm 118:1-2, 16-17, 22-23; Colossians 3:1-4
  or 1 Corinthians 5:6b-8; John 20:1-9

One of the Christian notions about God that has special meaning for anyone concerned about endangered human life is the idea that God is Creator of the universe. Begin at the beginning: it all comes from God (Gen 1:1).

If we really believe that God made it all and keeps the world going (Acts 17:28), then the believer is simply a caretaker, not the owner of natural resources. We are trustees, managers of the limited land, air, and water; caretakers, not undertakers.

For Christians, God gives all good things (Jas 1:17) and expects the recipient to make good use of them. How ironic, then, that some emotionally defend their doctrine of God as Creator in a pulpit harangue delivered in a wastefully air-conditioned auditorium to an overstuffed people, who, after church, drive their gas-guzzling SUVs to a restaurant for big, juicy steaks. If, indeed, God is Creator, this affects the way God's people live. They ask, "Am I supporting famine in the way I use God's gifts?" A related idea is that God alone is worthy of worship (Exod 20:3). The first of the Ten Commandments prohibits worship of any other deity but the Lord. For all practical purposes, there is an idolatry of narrow nationalism (America, love it or leave it) and a form of materialism (does it pay?) that take God's place in many people's lives.

Some of those studying world hunger have reduced the problems to economic projections. Overreliance on the study of economics (economism) is no less idolatry than the implicit belief that science has all the answers (scientism). One idolatry is as bad as another.

What is there about God's nature that helps us know how to respond to hungry people? God is a moral Person, not an abstract principle. God is just and righteous and holy and "light" (1 John 1:5) and "love" (1 John 4:8), sovereign God of the universe, yet also a caring Father. Believing that human beings are made in God's image (Gen 1:27) is so important that any difference between one person and another is relatively insignificant. Not enough has been made of the belief that all persons individually are created like God and capable of responding to the divine imperative (Psalm 8). Julius K. Nyerere, once president of Tanzania, said: "We say man was created in the image of God. I refuse to imagine a God who is miserable, poor, ignorant, superstitious, fearful, oppressed and wretched—which is the lot of the majority of those He created in His own image."[1]

This teaching that humans are made in God's image invests in individuals a worth and dignity that allow no easy escape from ethical responsibility. After all, each one is a replica of God. Norman Cousins said it well:

> Desensitization, not hunger, is the greatest curse on earth. It begins by calibrating people's credentials to live and ends by cheapening all life. . . . Famine in India and Bangladesh is a test not just of our capacity to respond as human beings, but of our ability to understand the cycles of civilization. We can't ignore out-stretched hands without destroying that which is most significant in the American character—a sense of vital identification with human beings wherever they are. Regarding life as the highest value is more important to the future of America than anything we make or sell.[2]

The Christian understanding of being made in God's image includes the oneness of the human family. Belief in the solidarity of the human

---

1. *The Radical Bible* (New York: Orbis Books, 1974).
2. Norman Cousins, *Saturday Review* (March 8, 1975) 4.

race, a prominent theme in Scripture, has been slighted. John Donne's "No man is an island . . . any man's death diminishes me, because I am involved in mankind" sounds very much like Paul's "We do not live to ourselves, and we do not die to ourselves" (Rom 14:7). Most Christian sympathies would be with G. K. Chesterton, who said, "We are all in a small boat on a stormy sea and we owe each other a terrible loyalty." Both our value and our oneness come from the very Nature of God.

Can you imagine a follower of Jesus Christ praying, "Give me this day my daily bread?" We need to make flesh those sentiments of solidarity.

Children's Time [LH]

Mention to the children that there's a phrase adults sometimes use that says, "Life goes on." We usually say that when we're facing a problem that's hard to overcome, yet we know that we have to move on and keep living day by day, even if our lives are more difficult. On Easter, though, the phrase "Life goes on" is a joyful one—it says that God has raised Jesus from death and that God loves us forever. God's love and life are meant to be shared, and that's why we happily reach out to those in need, so that all our lives can be full.

Musical Suggestions [LH]

Now the Green Blade Rises—LBW 148

Christ Is Alive—UMH 318

Praise the Living God Who Sings—BP 118

Because You Live, O Christ—NCH 231

Amy Booker-Hirsch

Second Sunday of Easter

RCL: Acts 2:14a, 22-32; Psalm 16; 1 Peter 1:3-9; John 20:19-31
LM: Acts 2:42-47; Psalm 118:2-4, 13-15, 22-24; 1 Peter 1:3-9;
   John 20:19-31

My North American church experience pales in comparison with the vibrant and alive spirit I experienced in the late 1980s in the African nation of Zaire, now known as the Democratic Republic of Congo. In a country known for its dismal human rights record and its low ranking on quality of life indices, the church is full and the services vibrant, alive, and open to the Spirit. This is quite different from our typical North American scenario of a 2.7-mile drive to a climate-controlled church with mauve pew cushions. As I returned from Africa to the U.S., the Holy Spirit seemed sadly lacking in our worship.

In today's passage from Acts, the author's focus is on the Holy Spirit and the organizational structure entailed in pouring out the Holy Spirit upon all flesh. Peter's speech treats us to David's prophetic account of the Messiah—the Anointed One! Peter proclaims that Jesus is the one to whom David refers. This Anointed One will come and bring new life. The early Church opened itself to Christ even when "the powers that be" were against it. As a matter of survival, the early Church also opened itself to the Spirit.

In today's Gospel Jesus appears to his disciples after his death. His words are powerful: "Peace be with you. As the Father has sent me, so I send you" (v. 21). Breathing on them, he says, "Receive the Holy

Spirit" (v. 22). In the passage from Acts, forgiveness of sins truly releases Peter's listeners to be about the work of Christ Jesus in founding the Christian Church. The Holy Spirit is poured out upon them so that they can see and hear. The early Church saw and heard and went and told.

What keeps us, as North Americans, from seeing and hearing the Holy Spirit in our day and time? For us, the Holy Spirit is the least understood and most forgotten Person of the Trinity. Perhaps we could take a lesson from our Asian, African, and Latin American brothers and sisters. Without many possessions in their "way," they truly are "The Way." Able to turn themselves over to the in-filling of the Spirit, they are willing to be the "beloved community," because they understand that the Holy Spirit is pouring forth upon them. They in turn let the power surge through them and in them and with them.

I know I had to let the "power" surge through me just to make it through a church service when I arrived in Zaire (Congo). It began with three hours in a packed church with no modern conveniences— just heat, humidity, and the Spirit. The offering was not a quiet passing of the plates. NOOO! It was a huge dance with the men on one side of the church and the women on the other. The line of dancers moved up and down along the aisles, often going outside. The offering alone took an hour. People counted the money right there on the spot, while the dancing continued. I had never experienced a scene involving people with literally nothing dancing and giving themselves to God. Slowly I began to "get" it. Attending worship is not about mauve pew cushions. It is about being community, humble and open to the Spirit. It's about God sending us, releasing us from old ways of being and making us new.

Prayer: Spirit God, make me new, open to your power to truly be released from old, stagnant ways. Amen.

Children's Time

Focus: John 20:19-31

It's right after Easter, and Jesus is alive, but he hasn't visited the disciples yet. They're all sad, and they don't think they can carry on Jesus' work without him to encourage them. They're also afraid, thinking, "The people who killed Jesus will soon be after us!" That would scare me! How does it make you feel? (Solicit answers.)

In fact, the disciples are in a locked room, and who comes to visit? (Let children respond.) Jesus comes! He knows they're sad and afraid, and he comes to bring them peace, which he does in a remarkable way. (Breathe on the children.) That's right—Jesus breathes on his disciples!

Jesus then talks to them about forgiving the sins of others and holding on to the sins of others. When we don't forgive the sins of others, it hurts us and hurts others. Do you like it when someone in your family or one of your friends says something like, "I'm not going to share my gum with you. You didn't share with me last time." Actions like that hurt our feelings, and they also hurt the person who is holding on to being mad. The disciples will have to learn to forgive.

Let's all take a big breath and then let it go. (Have the group do this twice.) This breathing starts to calm us down and make us peaceful. Jesus breathed on his disciples so they could start to calm down and so they would begin to be filled with the Spirit. They have a busy time ahead as they begin to build Christ's Church. They need all the calmness and Spirit they can get!

Prayer: Breathe on us, God, so we will be inspired to do your work. Amen.

Musical Suggestions [LH]

Spirit of the Living God (Response Chant)—BP 103

Breathe on Me, Breath of God—BP 88

Holy Spirit, Truth Divine—UMH 465

Draw Us in the Spirit's Tether—PH 504

O Breath of Life—UMH 543

Amy Booker-Hirsch

Third Sunday of Easter

RCL: Acts 2:14a, 36-41; Psalm 116:1-4, 12-19; 1 Peter 1:17-23;
Luke 24:13-35

LM: Acts 2:14, 22-33; Psalm 16:1-2, 5, 7-8, 9-10, 11; 1 Peter 1:17-21;
Luke 24:13-35

The Central American refugee walked across Honduras and made his way into Mexico. During Miguel's journey he was beaten, robbed by the "coyotes" who were to help him cross the border, and left for dead. Found and taken to Sister Cecelia in Nogales, he then came to Southside Presbyterian Church in Tucson, Arizona, where he was clothed, fed, and loved. Amy and Marianna worked on his asylum case. He got a green card, worked in a Tucson restaurant, and slept on Southside's floor. Grateful to God! That was Miguel!

In Central America, Miguel lived in conditions that were very similar to those of first-century Palestine. His government was hostile, and economic conditions devastated poor people, who could barely survive. When they tried to plant gardens or have a community school, people like Miguel were beaten and imprisoned. After all, "It's best not to let these peasants get too smart and figure out what the government is doing." His torture wounds truly reminded me of Christ's wounds from the cross. The believers in Acts were acting on their faith, just like Miguel, witnessing to the Christ crucified and resurrected.

Latin American crucifixes show a bloody, suffering Christ. Well, go figure! Bloodshed has been a part of these countries' histories. Central to their people's faith is the suffering Christ who persevered and triumphed over the cross. That is a Savior to whom they can all relate.

So the lesson from Acts sounds with a mighty ring to the lived experience of many around the globe. The Miguels of the world have it right: they intimately know the crucified Christ who bears the pain of systemic evil so that all of us might know new life. He truly wanted to save himself from a "corrupt generation."

I bet Miguel would have recognized Jesus on the road to Emmaus. He would not have to talk about Jesus being the "one who would redeem Israel." He knew Jesus did redeem and would continue to do so. Ada María Isasi-Díaz is a well-known theologian in Mujerista theology, which invites us to know and encounter God in the lived experience and stories of Latin American women (and I would add men and children too). A book she has written is filled with stories describing the living Christ, known in the breaking of tortillas. Her book is poignantly entitled *En la Lucha (In the Struggle): Elaborating a Mujerista Theology*.[1] Delightfully, the stories are in Spanish and English.

Prayer: Let us be on the way, Holy One, with the One whom we recognize and who in turn recognizes us. Amen.

Children's Time

Focus: Luke 24:13-35

Be prepared to act out the Emmaus story by walking around the sanctuary, or if not, to set the scene through a story. Have a portable mike, a helper to dim lights, someone to be Jesus, a blanket and bread and cups, and some simple costumes for the children as they enter the sanctuary as the service begins. After the children gather, invite them to walk with you and to talk about Jesus, just as the disciples would have in the time after Jesus died. Tell them: I'm really amazed by

---

1. Ada María Isasi-Díaz, *En la Lucha (In the Struggle): Elaborating a Mujerista Theology* (Minneapolis: Augsburg Fortress, 1993).

Jesus—aren't you? He was so wise telling us about his life and why he came. He told us things in stories we could understand about the sheep and goats, the house built on a rock instead of sand, and the woman who searched high and low for the lost coin. Do you like Jesus' stories?

But I never liked it when Jesus told us he must die. I just wouldn't listen. And now I'm sad, because he really is gone.

(Have the person you selected to be Jesus enter and say: "What are you all talking about?")

You say, "Don't you know? We were talking about Jesus of Nazareth, the one we hoped would be the Messiah, the one to save Israel! Some women in the village say they went to the tomb and he was not there. You must be the only person in Jerusalem not to know what's been happening these last few days."

Jesus: "I know that the Messiah would suffer before coming into glory. Let me tell you about Moses and all the prophets." (Pretend to talk between the two of you. Keep walking, and, if possible, dim the lights.) You say: "Let's stop, because it's getting late. Won't you stay with us, stranger?"

Jesus: "Yes, I'd like that."

(Lay out blankets, bread and cups, prepare to eat.)

Jesus (taking the bread): "This is my body, broken for you. Take and eat."

(You, as the leader, open your eyes wide. Jesus leaves.)

You say: "Wow, my heart was filled as I walked with this man. He explained the Scriptures to us as well. It was Jesus. Let's return and tell the others that Jesus has risen indeed!" (Lead the group back up front, shouting, "He is risen indeed!")

Prayer: God, thank you for Jesus' coming to the two disciples on the road. Let us recognize Jesus as he breaks bread and shares it with us. Amen.

Musical Suggestions [LH]

I Come with Joy—CH 420

Bread of the World, in Mercy Broken—CH 387

Here in This Place—GC 839

Christ Has Risen—GC 451

Amy Booker-Hirsch

▪

Fourth Sunday of Easter

▪

RCL: Acts 2:42-47; Psalm 23; 1 Peter 2:19-25; John 10:1-10

LM: Acts 2:14a, 36-41; Psalm 23:1-3a, 3b-4, 5, 6; 1 Peter 2:20b-25; John 10:1-10

The fields of wheat truly were "amber waves of grain." It was something to live in rural Oklahoma. The morning walks with my six-month-old in his sling were never the same. We saw farmhouses, cows, miles and miles of wheat, and blue sky. Most of all, I thought of the people who farmed the land. Their parents or grandparents had made the 1894 Land Run, seeking part of the last piece of unclaimed land in the continental United States. All a family had to do was line up and run as the whistle blew. The land they claimed was theirs for a dollar an acre.

In many cases the land was virtually worthless for farming. Yet some Mennonites introduced the hard red winter wheat of Russia. Conditions on the Oklahoma plains proved to be a good match for this hardy grain. The people who claimed the land were also hardy and from "all over the place." That's where we find ourselves in today's text from Acts, where we catch a glimpse of the make-up of the early Church. Despite their differences, they all have one thing in common: they find themselves in this one place with work to do, much like those early Oklahomans.

Peter urges these Christians to be about the work of repentance. "Turn around and go the other way" is how the word "repentance" translates. Sharing all things in common is a good first assignment for repentant ones, to dovetail with their duties of teaching, breaking bread, and praying together. The Church learned to be response-able—able to make a response in tandem with the Holy Spirit.

Psalm 23 is today's Psalter lesson. It poses many questions in light of hunger and poverty in our world. Who is shepherding us as a nation, as a body of believers? Are we as a nation aware of those who want? Where are the green pastures? The still waters? What restoration do we truly seek for ourselves, our nation, the world, our planet?

Each day many individuals walk through our "modern" dark valleys, facing structural evil that is none of their doing. Poor people do not get bogged down in status—at least not those I've met in Oklahoma, in Central America, or in Zaire (Congo). They know God loves them and comforts them. People who are poor know how to set a table and celebrate even on the midst of enemies. Perhaps a warring nation or a hateful neighbor is present at the table. Nonetheless, those who are poor show an astounding, lavish hospitality. Such hospitality in the midst of hate is no easy feat. It is something from which the world can learn.

Friends, come to the table. Mercy and goodness start here and dwell with us as we travel onward and offer hospitality to others.

Prayer: Lavish Host, we come as guests but also to help you at table. You invite us and we in turn beckon others. When all share, there is enough sustenance for all! This is cause for thankful celebration! Amen.

Children's Time

Focus: Acts 2:42-47

Bring a sheaf of wheat if possible. If not, get some grains of hard red winter wheat from a healthfood store. Also bring a world map.

Show the wheat, and tell the children that wheat like this is grown in Russia. Note where that is on the map. Remind them that it's cold there, and this wheat was made to survive in that cold. When people came from there to cold places in our country, they brought their wheat. Then note on the map where Oklahoma, Kansas, Nebraska, and Missouri are. Tell the children that people from all over the world came to settle there, and people still come from many places to the United States.

In today's story in Acts, people from all over are gathered together. They've decided to follow Jesus and be Christians. They share everything they have—money, food, and homes. They don't keep anything important just for themselves. They also pray together. People join with them, more and more each year, because they all want to live in community.

Like the wheat that could stand up to the cold, the Church had to be very strong to survive the things that came its way. It had to deal with people who hated the Church, and with bad weather, shipwrecks, hunger, and thirst. But the Church survived by trusting and believing in God. Many of the early settlers in our country did the same: they believed in God. As Christians today, we have many good examples to follow.

Prayer: God of all good things, thank you for the strong winter wheat that gives us bread. Thank you for the strong early Christians and early settlers of our own land, who show us how to keep going when life is not easy. Amen.

Musical Suggestions [LH]

You Satisfy the Hungry Heart—GC 815

Abundant Life—GC 710

How Like a Gentle Spirit—UMH 115

You Are Mine—FWS 2218

Amy Booker-Hirsch

Fifth Sunday of Easter

RCL: Acts 7:55-60; Psalm 31:1-5, 15-16; 1 Peter 2:2-10; John 14:1-14
LM: Acts 6:1-7; Psalm 33:1-2, 4-5, 18-19; 1 Peter 2:4-9; John 14:1-12

From 1985 to 1989 I wrote to a prisoner on death row in Arizona. I went to visit him the few times I was in Arizona. I felt so overwhelmed by the prison, the series of places to which I was escorted and in which I waited. This prisoner really wanted someone to befriend him. He wrote constantly, his letters always full of grammatical errors. He had not even finished grade school. His letters were needy. "Send me money. Send me your picture. Please give my name to others who can write me." I was guiltily relieved when I was called to serve overseas. I wrote a letter to the prisoner saying I was going out of the country and would not be available. Whew!

Imagine how Stephen's murderers feel as they stone him. "No longer will we have to listen to this call to repent and follow the life of Christ." They forget that you can get rid of the messenger but never the message. The message that all are forgiven and made whole was sorely needed in Stephen's day and time, yet Stephen's prophetic words were not taken well by those in power.

Prophetic voices that say "NO to death!" are sorely needed in our day and time. Sister Helen Prejean's prophetic voice says just such a NO to death. Her story of befriending a prisoner on death row is powerful because it takes a lot of guts to put a live face to a prison number. That's what Sister Prejean has done and continues to do as she reaches out both to victims' families and to their perpetrators' families.

Sister Prejean's story of intimacy with death row begins when Chava Colon, from the Prison Coalition in Louisiana, asks her to be a pen-pal for one of the men on death row in the state. She is already serving poor people in St. Thomas, a housing project in New Orleans, which she describes in her book, *Dead Man Walking,* as "not death row exactly, but close. Death is rampant here—from guns, disease, addiction." After Chava writes down the name of the death row inmate, he says, "Maybe I ought to give you someone else. This guy is a loner and doesn't write. Maybe you want someone who will answer your letters." But Sister Prejean replies and then reflects: "Don't change it. Give me his name." She writes: "I don't know yet the name on this tiny slip of white paper will be my passport into an eerie land that so far I've only read about in books."[1]

Sister Prejean gets the name Elmo Patrick Sonnier, No. 95281, Death Row, Louisiana State Penitentiary, Angola. Her compassion for and accompaniment of Sonnier is what Stephen needed as he died. Today's Gospel text from John fits for those who face the uncertain end of their lives on death row. "Do not let your hearts be troubled" (v. 1). Of course, the disciples just don't get it. People like Patrick Sonnier and the prisoner I visited get it. People who live with the guillotine poised over their neck every day either give up or find that death in this life is the way to God. The disciples and humanity today find that kind of knowledge elusive. The disciples had the privilege of witnessing what Jesus did and said, but they don't understand Christ until after he has left them.

Death row inmates often leave this world before the end of their natural lives. They cling fast to the knowledge of God's love that will take them beyond their seemingly miserable existence. In this is hope. They ask for things in God's name and receive, not as humanity would imagine it, but their prayers are answered.

Prayer: Knowledgeable One, may we learn more this day from those who face death. In death is life. Amen!

---

1. Sister Helen Prejean, C.S.J., *Dead Man Walking* (New York: Random House, 1993) 3, 4.

Children's Time

Focus: John 14:1-14

There's a story about a young boy who had a pet bug named Addie. One day the bug died and the boy was very sad. He wondered what he could have done differently so that the bug would still be alive. His father said, "Don't worry! There are lots of bugs. We'll get another one after church." But the boy piped right up and told his dad, "Yes, but it won't be Addie!"

That was a good answer. You see, the disciples in today's story are sad too. Jesus just told them that he is going away, to a place they cannot go. Thomas says he doesn't know where Jesus is going or the way he is going. Jesus patiently tells them that he (Jesus) is the way to God. If they know him, they will know God also. Then there is Philip, who wants to be shown God, and then he will be happy. Jesus again patiently explains that if they know Jesus, then they know God. But they just don't believe it will be the same as having Jesus and also having God with them. It is like they are saying, "Yes, but it won't be Jesus! Yes, but it won't be God!" Jesus tells them that he and God are one.

To that young boy I spoke about before, Addie was unique! Another bug just cannot replace her. For the disciples and for us, Jesus is unique. He can't just be replaced. So God sends the Holy Spirit to dwell in each person who loves Jesus. By doing this, his disciples are able to carry on Jesus' work. Even when their hearts are troubled, they can do God's and Jesus' work because the Spirit is with them.

Prayer: Comfort us, God, when our hearts are sad. Give us patience to follow in Jesus' way with the Spirit guiding us. Amen.

Musical Suggestions [LH]

Christ Is the Truth, the Way—BP 179

Come, My Way, My Truth, My Life—LBW 513

Christ Is Made the Sure Foundation—NCH 400

O Praise the Gracious Power—NCH 54

Amy Booker-Hirsch

Sixth Sunday of Easter

RCL: Acts 17:22-31; Psalm 66:8-20; 1 Peter 3:13-22; John 14:15-21
LM: Acts 8:5-8, 14-17; Psalm 66:1-3, 4-5, 6-7, 16, 20; 1 Peter 3:15-18;
    John 14:15-21

Jack Nelson-Pallmeyer, in his book *Hunger for Justice*, writes about walking the streets of Calcutta, India, and recognizing this hard truth: "In the suffering of the poor, God was screaming at me, in fact at all of us and at our institutions and social systems that cause and perpetuate hunger, poverty, and inequality."[1] Walter Wink, citing this quote, continues on this same theme in his book *The Powers That Be: Theology for a New Millennium:* "We end, then, with that divine cry ringing in our ears, exhorting us to engage these mighty Powers in the strength of the Holy Spirit, that human life might become more fully human."[2]

In today's passage from Acts 17, the apostle Paul "screams" at us to be about God's work. The altar to an unknown god in Athens unsettles him. The altars to "known gods" in our day should unsettle us! Can we name a few? The automobile, a meal in five minutes, even modern plumbing and lights? God "commands all people everywhere to repent" (v. 30). Here are some ways to start repenting! Is walking

---

1. Jack Nelson-Pallmeyer, *Hunger for Justice* (Maryknoll, N.Y.: Orbis Books, 1980) vii.
2. Walter Wink, *The Powers That Be: Theology For a New Millennium* (New York: Galilee Doubleday, 1998) 199.

to church an option? How about fasting? How about a prayer meeting devoted just to prayers for the world's poor people? The possibilities for our work of dismantling "institutions and social systems that cause and perpetuate hunger, poverty, and inequality" abound. God can start with you and dismantle your own prejudices about those who are poor. If the first-century Christians could do it in the face of great persecution, why can't we?

John's Gospel text today, a text often used at funerals, gives us some help when it comes to living in the Spirit. After all, the disciples are asked to start "making the break" from Jesus. Jesus himself knows his death is near. But the disciples don't understand that yet. Without Jesus embodied, working with them and next to them, what can they expect? Jesus' use of the word "Counselor" translates as "one called to work alongside." Jesus points the disciples toward the future as he presses the point that he and the Spirit are one.[3]

Look to the future with and in the Spirit. Pentecost is near, but more importantly, the Spirit is here, in you and in all. Take the time to begin the season by drinking in the Spirit. Do not stop there. Dwell in the Spirit. The Spirit of God, as Wink so poignantly states, exhorts us "to engage these mighty Powers in the strength of the Holy Spirit, that human life might become more fully human."

Prayer: Breathe on us, God. Dismantle our fear that no one will like us if we preach the Good News. We need a "good talkin' to" from you so that we might claim our complicity in a "privileged world." Guide us to take bold actions in the Spirit to unravel one thread at a time the "coat of privilege" we wear. Alleluia! Amen!

Children's Time

Focus: Acts 17:22-31

Bring pictures of a nation in famine or in the distress of war. Ask the children what they see. They will say "hungry people," "war," or "hurt," etc. Ask what they think we can do to help. (Solicit responses, and supplement their answers with things like "Send money," "Pray," "Go on a mission trip," or support Bread for the World or your faith tradition's hunger appeal.)

3. D. Moody Smith, *Harper's Bible Commentary* (San Francisco: Harper and Row, 1988) 1068.

When Paul visited the early church in Athens, Greece, he saw that there were many idols for them to worship instead of the one true God. He said, "God made the earth and all peoples so that we can look for and find God. We are God's children. We ought not to make gods of stone. We need to repent and be sorry for what we have done so we can be made to live again."

What the people in Greece had done really bothered Paul. He believed they were putting their own wishes for themselves ahead of what God wished for them. What do you think God wishes for us today? (Gather answers.) Do you think God wants us to be concerned about people everywhere or just about ourselves? (Allow answers.)

God wants us to care for people in Afghanistan, in Iraq, in Congo, in Palestine and Israel, and in our own country. In fact, we are called to care for all people, all animals, plants, and nature everywhere.

I liked your suggestions earlier on how to help these people in the pictures. How did you know what to do? (Listen to the children's comments. All answers are great. Perhaps someone will say "the Holy Spirit" or "God." If not, lead the discussions toward the Holy Spirit.)

Remember how we have talked about God in each one of us, helping us to know the right thing to do. This is the Holy Spirit. The time in the Church when the Holy Spirit visited the early Christians is coming. The day is called Pentecost. We celebrate it each year to remind us how important the Spirit is in our lives.

Prayer: Our one true God, show us how to live in the Spirit so we may repent of our ways and go your Way. Amen.

Musical Suggestions [LH]

The Lord Hears the Cry of the Poor—BP 109

God Our Author and Creator—NCH 530

O God in Heaven—NCH 279

Now Praise the Hidden God of Love—PH 402

Amy Booker-Hirsch

The Ascension of the Lord

RCL: Acts 1:1-11; Psalm 47 or Psalm 93; Ephesians 1:15-23; Luke 24:44-53

LM: Acts 1:1-11; Psalm 47:2-3, 6-7, 8-9; Ephesians 1:17-23; Matthew 28:16-20

Okay, who's in and who's out? There is an ongoing flight of Central Americans and Mexicans through the Sonoran desert and eventually to hoped-for freedom in the United States of America. Their plight gives a modern-day angle to the quarrel in the early Church about who is clean and unclean. My friend Robin Hoover, pastor of First Christian Church, Disciples of Christ, in Tucson, Arizona, clearly sees it his mission to save anyone who might perish in the desert from heat and dehydration while seeking a chance at freedom. His creation of Humane Borders grows and thrives. Humane Borders seeks to make the Arizona-Mexico border humane. It offers clean water and has people of good conscience patrolling and aiding refugees. Upon their safe arrival, the United States government can deal with the legality of who's in and who's out. But Humane Borders believes that no one should perish in the desert in hopes of attaining freedom. "We must take death out of the immigration equation," Robin says.

Clearly, Robin welcomes the refugees, engages in table fellowship, and makes a place for them in the community. Robin sees them as "good" and vital to the community in southern Arizona. Perhaps there are critics at your places of worship saying things like, "If the congregant does not speak English, if the congregant has not had a bath, if the congregant brings a less-than-appetizing dish to the monthly potluck . . ." You get the idea; these are "in or out" questions.

Jesus speaks of this when he says, "There are other sheep that do not belong to this fold. I must bring them also, and they will listen to my voice" (John 10:16). The Good News must go to the Gentiles as well. Post-Easter, pre-Pentecost fans, "Beware of the Spirit in your midst. It has been unleashed and more power is coming!"

Perhaps on the road to Hermosillo or Magdalena in northern Mexico, in the state of Sonora, you will be treated to meeting Jesus "on the way." I know my Central American friends recognize him as they walk in the Spirit of freedom. Jesus is the one who breaks tortillas with them. It is then they recognize him. Maybe I'm a bit out of line, but I truly see Robin as being Christ to so many. The Protestant reformer Martin Luther admonished us to be "little Christs to one another." Way to go, Robin! I nominate you as a "little Christ"!

But Robin is not ascending to heaven. Rather, Robin is bringing a bit of heaven to earth, where the glimpse of God's realm is desperately needed. So as you celebrate Ascension of the Lord, don't crane your neck too hard looking up. Rather, look around and see the face of Jesus in the grocery store clerk, the bank teller, the refugee from Guatemala. Oh, and stay close to the Spirit!

Prayer: The acts of present-day disciples are ascending and descending all around us, Gracious One. Grounded in humble demonstrations of care, we see and give thanks for your Son's presence among us.

Children's Time

Focus: Acts 1:1-11

Dress in first-century garb, and, as you enter, pretend to look over your shoulder. Act afraid! Tell the children that some people are after you because you worship Jesus, and you are very afraid. (Hide behind the kids, who are up front, or if possible some congregants out in the sanctuary.)

Ask the children if they know why you are so afraid? (Solicit responses. Again, hopefully someone will say it is because you are a Christian, and the authorities are searching for those who follow Jesus so that they can get rid of them. If no one says anything like this, then guide the discussion that way.)

Tell the children: "I'm terrified that the people who killed Jesus will kill me too because I am his follower. What I wouldn't do for some courage! I asked Jesus to tell me when he might restore the kingdom of Israel, but he said it was not for me to know. Then he talked all about this Holy Spirit that would come upon his followers. I actually was a little bit upset. I wanted him to tell me when and how God's kingdom was going to come. If all of his followers are going to receive this 'Holy Spirit' power, then I guess it's up to us to restore the kingdom. That's what has me afraid!

"Just as Jesus was talking to us, he was lifted up into the clouds. I couldn't believe it! He is not going to be with us as we go and spread God's word. Here I was, gawking, looking up into the clouds when two dazzling white messengers told us, 'People of Galilee, why do you stand looking up into heaven? This Jesus, who has been taken up from you into heaven, will come in the same way as you saw him go into heaven.'

"I guess I should get busy doing the work Jesus called me to do. I sure am scared of what this work will mean, and especially of the Holy Spirit. Yet I remember how Jesus said he would be with us just a little bit longer and then would send the Comforter. Maybe this Holy Spirit will give me the courage I need to go and tell about Jesus! Let's pray for some of that courage!"

Prayer: We wait for courage, God, knowing that you are with us to do your work in all places and at all times! Thank you! Amen!

Musical Suggestions [LH]

Come to Us—GC 743

All Are Welcome—GC 753

God is Here!—CH 280

Eternal Christ, You Rule—NCH 302

Amy Booker-Hirsch

▦

Seventh Sunday of Easter

▦

RCL: Acts 1:6-14; Psalm 68:1-10, 32-35; 1 Peter 4:12-14; 5:6-11;
    John 17:1-11
LM: Acts 1:12-14; Psalm 27:1, 4, 7-8; 1 Peter 4:13-16; John 17:1-11a

Pentecost is one church holiday unscathed by North American commercialism! That is, right after Easter, I do not see "Happy Pentecost"
decorations up in malls or in town halls. Many Christians have to think
hard about what Pentecost means. I know I drilled into my confirmands
that it is truly a celebration of the Church. I think they got the idea!
They even knew it arrived 50 days after Easter, so it was on a different
day every year according to the lunar calendar.

So get the Pentecost decorations out now! This is going to be one
"spirited" holy day. Did you read that right? I hope so! Because Pentecost has not been co-opted by commercialism, whereas Christmas and
Easter have no semblance to the original holy days celebrating Christ
in our lives. But Pentecost remains a day to celebrate the Holy Spirit.

Remember that the disciples are hiding for fear of being crucified
for being Christ's followers. I doubt that the disciples remember Jesus'
words that he would be with them yet just a little while, that where he
is going they cannot go. More potent is the fact that he tells them not
to be troubled, because one is coming who will comfort and empower
them. They have post-traumatic stress disorder, a real condition that
affects people who have experienced loss and grief.

So embrace the disciples as truly human, with issues of loss and grief
just like people today. Take them off the "holy shelf" and place them
in the ebb and flow of life just like you know it. It is then that the Bible

becomes a living book, full of people who are just like us. Yet they persevere in the Spirit—faithful, albeit not perfect.

The disciples in today's text from Acts want the kingdom of Israel restored! Furthermore, they want to know when that is going to happen. They haven't yet received the Spirit, so they are in the dark. They keep looking up for Jesus. Not to give Jesus' followers a bum rap for all that they do or don't do; they do some things very well. Case in point: they include women in Christ's followers and they devote themselves to prayer.

John's Gospel text treats us to Jesus' sympathy and compassion for his followers as he prays fervently for them. It is edifying to know that Jesus understands that they cannot be taken out of the world, so he asks God to protect them from the evil that is rampant and pervasive in the world of that time.

Both Protestant and Catholic epistle passages underscore what emotional, physical, mental, and spiritual distress is at hand for those who claim Christ and Christ's Church. To bear the name Christian in that era meant suffering—a far cry from where most of us find ourselves in North America.

So get the candles ready, the streamers and confetti too. The fear, alienation, and evil swirling in the air as the disciples wait for further instructions are just around the corner. Centuries later, we have the knowledge of what happened on Pentecost to free the Church. Yet we still often live cowardly lives in light of the Spirit. It's never too late to claim the "Spirit of God" resting on us.

Prayer: Spirit One, reveal to us that which we need to do to live in the Spirit. Amen.

Children's Time [LH]

Remind the children that Jesus loved his disciples very dearly. The prayer Jesus prays in today's passage from John is a poignant reminder of how much he wanted his disciples to be one, unified in spirit and actions, and how they now belonged to God and rested in God's protection. Use these words to assure the children they too are deeply loved—by Jesus, by their families, by those around them in the congregation. Invite the congregation to say aloud to the children, "We love you," and for the children to respond in the same way to the congregation.

Prayer: God, bless these young ones, just as Jesus asked that you bless and protect his disciples. Help us to be your loving people, working together for good. Amen.

Musical Suggestions [LH]

Born of God, Eternal Savior—NCH 542

Oh, Love, How Deep—LBW 88

Like the Murmur of the Dove's Song—UMH 544

Come and Find the Quiet Center—FWS 2128

Amy Booker-Hirsch

Pentecost Sunday

RCL: Acts 2:1-21 or Numbers 11:24-30; Psalm 104:24-34, 35b;
  1 Corinthians 12:3b-13 or Acts 2:1-21; John 20:19-23 or
  John 7:37-39
LM: Acts 2:1-11; Psalm 104:1, 24, 29-30, 31, 34; 1 Corinthians 12:3b-7,
  12-13; John 20:19-23

Everyone twittered. I read the passage in English. Then María, from
Paraguay, read the passage in Spanish. Twitters arose in the congregation. Andreas, from Germany, also read the Scripture. More twittering. It was a bit disconcerting to us! After all, we sat through worship
every Sunday listening to words in a tongue we did not understand.
But in a way we understood very well what was being said. It was
Pentecost in Bolenge, Zaire (now Congo), and the pastor wanted the
people to experience Acts 2:1-21 in different tongues.

I had done the same thing in the States, that is, read the Scriptures
in different languages. But what a difference it made when I was in the
minority. It was quite humbling to experience that twittering. In
retrospect, it was like God's presence at Sinai for me. Inspired speaking and hearing happened in that place, changing my usual inattention
into rapt attention as the Spirit spoke to me. God's deeds of power
were all around me. Power was in the wake I had attended for a small
baby the previous night. Power was in the AIDS patient for whom I
was cooking food, attempting to bring her some comfort in her final
days. Power was in the seemingly inane teaching of English to the

young people, many of whom would never leave this place of jungle heat and abject poverty.

What does all this mean? It was a question that the amazed and perplexed people asked on the day of the first Pentecost, a question that we all need to ask again in our own day. May inattention to the Spirit become rapt attention to the Spirit. The prophet Joel had it right in seeing the last days as Spirit-filled ones. Did you read the words "upon all flesh" (Acts 2:17)? The Spirit will reside in sons and daughters, in old men and young men, in slaves of both genders! The Church's exclusivity is challenged and thankfully broken at Pentecost, offering instead the Spirit's inclusivity. Well, it's about time we jumped on board the Spirit Wagon! The message for the early Church resounds in our ears today as the Church is called to include all races, socioeconomic circles, genders, children, gays, and lesbians.

Everyone understood the tongues, each in his or her own language. The language of the Spirit is one we all can understand. Peter's sermon focuses on renewal and on prophecy, urging the people to shun corruption, themes that fit for us today.

I attended a Bread for the World national gathering in June 2001 at Georgetown University in Washington, D.C. The prophetic words I heard and the relationships I experienced moved me. No longer would I be about "business as usual" in my North American mindset. I heard from Africans, Europeans, South Americans, North Americans—each in his or her own tongue—and I understood the Spirit. The modern-day prophets prophesied about drought, hunger, and disease, and described what I could do about them. They urged me to "repent," to turn around and go the other way. For me, that meant a lifestyle change and a Spirit-change. I admitted that I had become too attached to my house and car. I fasted more, rode my bike and took the bus more often, and spent time with my local Interfaith Council for Peace and Justice, where many people from across the globe gathered.

I hope everyone can have a "Pentecost" experience, whether big or little, dramatic or quiet. Be open to the Spirit in your life. Pentecost is a liturgical season that lends itself to focus on this "Person" of the Trinity. In all you do, hit your knees, seek humility, and "let go." Attention to the Spirit will change your life.

Prayer: God, send your Spirit again, powerfully, among us in all our diversity, so that we might experience your life-giving, unifying breath. Amen.

Children's Time

Focus: Acts 2:1-21

From construction paper cut out tongues of fire to give the children as they enter. Ask different people, in advance, to be prepared to emphatically say "Receive the Holy Spirit" in different languages. When you ask, have them say:

"Receive the Holy Spirit!" (English)

"Recibe el Espíritu Santo!" (Spanish)

"Recevez le Saint-Esprit!" (French)

Include other languages that congregants may know.

Then say to the children: "Wow! Isn't it great to hear the differences in languages? I sure like them! Remember how we have been talking about Jesus' followers receiving the Holy Spirit. We've been waiting! They've been waiting! Today's the DAY! Everyone was together in one place. And suddenly a big wind came up. Let's make the sound of a big wind [Have the children blow.] The wind filled the whole room. Next, tongues of fire rested on each person present! Hold your paper tongue over your head! [Have one for yourself to demonstrate and have the children follow your lead.]

"The Holy Spirit filled these early Christians. Everyone started to speak in different languages, just as our friends did earlier. All this was amazing! But more amazing was that everyone heard in his or her own native language. Everyone spoke! Everyone heard! Everyone understood! Now that's what was amazing!

"Today the Church is big, having spread around the world. We are Christians because the early Christians, who were once afraid of sharing the Good News, received the Holy Spirit, which gave them the power to do God's work. Now in our day and time, it is just as important to share our faith. How might we talk about Jesus with our friends? [Invite answers.] Great! Let's do these things! Today we say it's the Church's birthday, when people came out from behind locked doors with courage and Spirit to share the Good News! Let's pray!"

Prayer: Thank you, God, for the early Christians. They spoke! They heard! They understood, and then went and told others! Alleluia! Amen!

Musical Suggestions [LH]

Holy Spirit, Truth Divine—UMH 465

Diverse in Culture, Nation, Race—GC 739

Wind Who Makes All Winds That Blow—UMH 538

Spirit Blowing through Creation—GC 462

Many and Great, O God, Are Thy Things—PH 271

William J. Byron, S.J.

Trinity Sunday

RCL: Genesis 1:1–2:4a; Psalm 8; 2 Corinthians 13:11-13;
   Matthew 28:16-20
LM: Exodus 34:4b-6, 8-9; Daniel 3:52, 53, 54, 55;
   2 Corinthians 13:11-13; John 3:16-18

An entire homily for this day can be built around a poem entitled
"Trinity Sunday" by the famous English poet George Herbert. He died
in 1633 and throughout his adult life was a country pastor. He wrote:

> Lord, who hast form'd me out of mud,
>   And hast redeem'd me through thy blood,
>   And sanctified me to do good;
>
> Purge all my sins done heretofore:
>   For I confess my heavy score,
>   And I will strive to sin no more.
>
> Enrich my heart, mouth, hands in me,
>   With faith, with hope, with charity;
>   That I may run, rise, rest with thee.[1]

Creator, Redeemer, Sanctifier—the one God in three Persons.
Creator: "Lord, who hast form'd me out of mud." *Redeemer:* "And
who hast redeem'd me through thy blood." *Sanctifier:* "And sanctified

---

1. John N. Wall, Jr., ed., *George Herbert: The Country Parson, The Temple* (New
York: Paulist Press, 1981) 184.

me to do good." In the third stanza the poet continues with three little "trinities," triplets of petitions that apply to anyone who hears these texts proclaimed today:

> Enrich my heart, mouth, hands in me,
>   With faith, with hope, with charity;
>   That I may run, rise, rest with thee.

Responding in a trinitarian way to the mystery of the Most Holy Trinity means first committing to serve God. It is a commitment of the whole self—heart, mouth, hands—to God, wherever and in whatever state and stage of life we exist by God's loving providence.

The heart: Does God have a place in our deepest longings? Is there room there for those who are hungry and powerless? Is there any distance now between our believing hearts and the heart of God? Is it possible for poor and hungry people to help bridge that gap?

The mouth: Do we speak like Christians, like followers of Christ? Or does our speech betray in us convictions that are not of God, far from God, opposed to God? Is speaking up and out for those who are poor a way of putting our mouths in proper alignment with trinitarian convictions? Bread for the World provides speaking-out and speaking-up opportunities for BFW members who meet with their congressional representatives and their staffs.

The hands: What are our believing hands doing for God? What have they done for God? What might they do for God in the days and months and years ahead? What might they be doing for poor people? The annual Bread for the World Offering of Letters campaign invites us to take pen in hand and let lawmakers know how their votes can help or hurt our poor neighbors.

Needed now is a triple response—heart, mouth, hands—to the call of the Most Holy Trinity. The poet would have us, as believers, pray to be enriched "with faith, with hope, with charity," the three-part treasury available to all by the grace of the Triune God. Faith, the act by which our lives are entrusted to God; hope, the conviction that sustains us when things appear to be desperate; charity, the love that knows no petty perimeter but reaches far beyond our self-interest to include hungry people and stretches still farther—all the way home to God.

This means being ready to "run, rise, and rest" with God. Run, rise, and rest. Where? To what purpose? This can be the rhythm of advocacy for poor and hungry people. Those verbs can stir the imagination to hear anew Jesus' words at the end of Matthew's Gospel: "Go therefore and make disciples of all nations, baptizing them in the name of the Father and of the Son and of the Holy Spirit, and teaching them to obey everything that I have commanded you" (vv. 19-20). Not the least of those commands is an attentive response to the cry of the poor.

Children's Time [LH]

Have the children look at their hands. What amazing things they are! Ask the children what we do with our hands. Note that we can write letters using our hands (a very useful point if your Offering of Letters occurs this day). We use all our senses—eyes, ears, mouth—and our hands to help others.

Musical Suggestions [LH]

Lord, You Give the Great Commission—BP 106

You Satisfy the Hungry Heart—GC 815

Now the Silence—GC 754

Lord, Speak to Me, That I May Speak—PH 426

Creative Lord, You Own the Fields—BP 159

Spirit of God—FWS 2117

Praise with Joy the World's Creator—NCH 273

William J. Byron, S.J.

Ninth Sunday in Ordinary Time

RCL: Genesis 6:9-22; 7:24; 8:14-19; Psalm 46; Romans 1:16-17;
3:22b-28 (29-31); Matthew 7:21-29

LM: Deuteronomy 11:18, 26-28; Psalm 31:2-3, 3-4, 17, 25;
Romans 3:21-25, 28; Matthew 7:21-27

Anyone concerned with the problem of world hunger will make special note of the Lord's instruction to Noah to "take with you every kind of food that is eaten, and store it up; and it shall serve as food for you and for them" (Gen 6:21). The "them" in this case includes Noah and his wife, his three sons and their wives, and two "of every living thing"—birds, animals, and every creeping thing. Quite a collection and quite a collective appetite for food! Noah gives new meaning to the word "provisioning."

The waters "swelled on the earth for one hundred fifty days," we are told, so the provisions had to last at least that long. It was not yet raining when Noah began to build the ark, which reminds us that planning ahead is related to survival. Famine, like flood, will destroy life. Provisioning, in the broadest sense of that word, must begin long before either famine or flood begins to take its toll.

Food reserves—international grain reserves—require both political will and appropriate agricultural technology. Neither, presumably, was much of an issue for Noah, who simply followed orders and built his floating storehouse to the Lord's specified dimensions: three hundred cubits by fifty cubits by thirty cubits. A "cubit," for those who might be wondering, is the length of an adult forearm from elbow to extended middle finger. The precise measurements are unimportant. The point is this: provisioning takes time, space, and serious commitment.

Gathering emergency food aid to avoid starvation is one thing; providing for an abundant future is quite another. The Christian conscience is concerned with both. Future food supplies depend on science, technology, political will, education, and diplomacy, as well as peace within and between nations.

To put a reverent twist on Matthew 7:21ff., "Not everyone who says to me, 'Lord, Lord,' will" have enough to eat. Prayer alone won't do it. Asking and waiting are not enough. Action is necessary. "[O]nly the one who does the will of my Father in heaven" is going to be part of the solution to the problem of world hunger. "Everyone who hears these words of mine and acts on them" is going to be of genuine assistance to those who are poor and hungry in this world.

According to a saying that used to make the rounds in Dorothy Day's Catholic Worker movement, "The trouble with the world is that the people who do all the thinking never act, and the people who do all the acting never think." What has been needed since the time of Noah, and what is particularly necessary in the face of worldwide hunger and poverty, is a combination of thought and action powerful enough to deal with huge societal problems. Where faith and works combine to shape both thought and action, provisioning strategies for the world's hungry poor people will be "founded on rock," the kind of rock that supports any faith community that wants to help.

Children's Time [LH]

Where do we store food as we plan ahead for future meals? In pantries, freezers, cupboards? Noah stored food so that he and those on board could survive, and we store food so we'll have enough to eat (though probably not 150 days' worth!). In today's world there are times when many people don't have enough to eat for a long time in one place, and so are at risk of dying—we call that a famine. Countries store up food to help when famine hits. We need to make sure that all God's people can be fed.

Musical Suggestions [LH]

How Firm a Foundation—NCH 407

Amazing Grace! How Sweet the Sound—BP 105

William J. Byron, S.J.

◾

Tenth Sunday in Ordinary Time

◾

RCL: Genesis 12:1-9; Psalm 33:1-12; Romans 4:13-25; Matthew 9:9-13, 18-26

LM: Hosea 6:3-6; Psalm 50:1, 8, 12-13, 14-15; Romans 4:18-25; Matthew 9:9-13

"Follow me." In describing the call to discipleship, Christians talk not only about hearing the call to follow Christ but about *being* a call—not so much having a vocation as being a vocation. This means trying to be always responsive and responding, always attuned to God's voice, always aligned with God's will. God's voice and will today, in a world wounded by poverty and hunger, are surely saying and willing that those who have must share, those who can must help.

Scripture states the reality of discipleship simply: Matthew gets up and follows Jesus. It's interesting that the first stop on this incipient journey of faith, this following of Christ, is a dinner table. Matthew hears the Pharisees ask why Jesus eats with tax collectors and sinners. He follows a leader who eats, a leader presumably sensitive to those who have no place at the table. Tax collectors were hated in those days because they were seen as agents of a foreign Roman power. Moreover, they had a way of enriching themselves unjustly at the expense of poor people. But they, too, in Jesus' view, deserve a place at the table.

All creation is a table God sets to meet the needs of men and women everywhere and at all times. Everyone has a faith-based human right to be there. The promise that Abraham and his descendants would inherit the world was not based in law but on the righteousness of faith, Paul says. Faith-committed Christians are called to do what they can to make sure that all their brothers and sisters in the human community (broadly speaking, the descendants of Abraham) receive their share of the inheritance, have their place at the table, and enjoy their portion of the meal.

That is the mission of Bread for the World. Advocacy is the BFW style. By their activism, Bread for the World members participate in that mission and demonstrate their fidelity to the call to discipleship.

As they leave church on Sundays, members of my former Washington, D.C., parish, Holy Trinity Catholic Church, pass under an overhead sign that reminds them of the challenge of Matthew 25. The sign asks, "Lord, when did we see you hungry?" On Monday mornings these worshipers go back to work on Capitol Hill, in the White House, in law firms, trade associations, and lobbying organizations and find themselves wondering how, from those observation posts, they can "see" and do something for poor and hungry people. Fifteen or twenty parishioners have met occasionally at Holy Trinity with BFW president David Beckmann to offer strategy advice and enlist congressional cosponsors for legislation that Bread for the World is trying to advance on Capitol Hill. Most recently, these parishioners made a difference in Congress's passing the "Africa: Hunger to Harvest" resolution and in the effort to help elected representatives see the moral urgency of making the TANF program (Temporary Assistance for Needy Families) more effective in lifting people out of poverty.

They don't say it in exactly these words, and perhaps don't formally think about it in these terms, but what these parishioners are doing is part of their response to the call all of us hear: "Follow me."

Children's Time [LH]

Energetically invite the children to follow you around the sanctuary. Stop and invite some adults in the congregation (who have been alerted beforehand) to come along as well. Have most come willingly, but have a couple resist before joining in. Soon you'll have a slightly raucous procession. Explain to the children that Jesus calls us to come and follow him. It's not always easy, but we need to respond in some way to his invitation. Suggest a few ways your church does justice as a way of following Jesus.

Musical Suggestions [LH]

We Are Called—FWS 2172

We Sing to You, O God—NCH 9

Let Us Hope when Hope Seems Hopeless—NCH 461

You Are Mine—FWS 2218

Whatsoever You Do—GC 670

William J. Byron, S.J.

■

Eleventh Sunday in Ordinary Time

■

RCL: Genesis 18:1-15 (21:1-7); Psalm 116:1-2, 12-19; Romans 5:1-8;
 Matthew 9:35–10:8 (9-23)

LM: Exodus 19:2-6a; Psalm 100:1-2, 3, 5; Romans 5:6-11;
 Matthew 9:36–10:8

 Those who grow discouraged in the face of persistent world hunger and poverty can find consolation in the story in Genesis 18 of Abraham and Sarah welcoming the three men the Lord sends them. In particular, verse 14 should sink into the soul, roll around the mind like a mantra, and be internalized as a guiding principle and deeply held conviction. "Is anything too wonderful for the Lord?" Cannot the Lord work any wonder? Is anything impossible for God? Yes, the Lord can work wonders. No, nothing is impossible for God. Why, then, does hunger persist? Because, we have to admit, God chooses to work with human hands. And humanity's hands, including our own, have not applied themselves effectively to the task of eliminating hunger and balancing the worldwide scales of justice.

If, as Matthew 10:7 reminds us, the kingdom of heaven was near, or at hand, when Jesus dispatched the Twelve to do his missionary work, why has the kingdom not yet been fully grasped? It is a reign, as we know, of justice and peace. Why have injustices been so widespread and peace so elusive through the twenty centuries from the day Christ declared the kingdom to be near? An honest answer to that question requires us to admit that we, and those who have gone before us, have neglected to reduce the barriers among and within ourselves to the coming of the promised kingdom. We tolerate injustice. We permit poverty.

I think of poverty as "sustained deprivation." People who are poor are deprived of many things, food being one of them. In the face of the promise of a coming kingdom of justice and peace, the question we ask ourselves is this: What is sustaining the deprivations that define the poverty of millions in the human family today? This in turn forces us to examine our ways of doing things, our systems and structures. Are they sinful? Is injustice built into the way we organize our relationships to one another, person to person, group to group, nation to nation?

We don't really know anything about the three men who visited Sarah and Abraham. Their mysterious presence in this story lets us speculate on the way God communicates with us, on who it might be today who carries God's messages to us, on the ways in which we might read God's will in the faces, words, and events surrounding us in the daily doings of life. But Abraham's and Sarah's response to the arrival of these men tells volumes. In the heat of the day and in their vulnerability, Sarah and Abraham share abundant food and drink and provide shelter. Their instincts are to offer hospitality and welcome, even to strangers. The men's word is one of radical blessing, even as Abraham and Sarah have shared the peace of the sustaining table.

Bread for the World is, I'm convinced, an instrument of the Lord's peace, a blessing. Bread for the World raises a prophetic voice of justice speaking to power. Bread for the World is working to reduce the barriers to the coming of the promised kingdom, which remains near but not yet grasped.

Children's Time [LH]

Remind children that families often invite others over for dinner, to share food and a good time. As we talk we learn more about the people we've invited. Abraham and Sarah invited people in because that was what people did in their time for people who had been on a hot, difficult journey. From those people Abraham and Sarah learned important information about themselves and their future. Maybe harsh weather and hard journeys are no longer the main reason we invite people into our homes, but whenever we show hospitality and share food and time with others, we learn important things. We are blessed.

Musical Suggestions [LH]

Awake, Awake to Love and Work—NCH 89

Come to Tend God's Garden—NCH 586

God It Was—GC 701

God, Whose Love Is Reigning o'er Us—UMH 100

As We Gather at Your Table—FWS 2268

William J. Byron, S.J.

Twelfth Sunday in Ordinary Time

RCL: Genesis 21:8-21; Psalm 86:1-10, 16-17; Romans 6:1b-11;
Matthew 10:24-39

LM: Jeremiah 20:10-13; Psalm 69:8-10, 14, 17, 33-35; Romans 5:12-15;
Matthew 10:26-33

The advocacy dimension of social justice ministry gives the Christian activist an opportunity to line up for the blessing Jesus promises in Matthew 10:32: "Everyone therefore who acknowledges me before others, I also will acknowledge before my Father in heaven." With the eye of faith, Christians see Jesus in poor and hungry people and acknowledge Jesus when they stand up for the rights of those who are marginalized. The right to food, the right to life, the right to shelter, employment, healthcare, education, and personal security—advocacy for all these rights acknowledges the person of Jesus present in those who lack those necessities.

All the elements needed to enjoy human dignity reflect the divine image in the human person. That image is defaced by hunger, poverty, and homelessness, to name just three contemporary assaults on human dignity. Advocacy on behalf of those trapped in these various deprivations amounts to acknowledging Christ "before others." The "others" are those who occupy seats of power, those who exercise influence, those who suffer the deprivations as well as those who cause them, and those who feel helpless and wonder why "something isn't being done to eliminate these problems." Something can be done, and Bread for the World is one of many Christian advocacy movements that prove it.

Executives sometimes complain that it's lonely at the top. Ask advocates whether they feel lonely in the middle of controversy, or on the front lines of confrontation, or toward the bottom of career-prestige rankings as they attempt to promote and protect the interests of poor people. It can be very lonely there. Social justice advocates need a supportive spirituality to shore up both their spirits and their staying power. One such spirituality is rooted in Matthew 10:39: "Those who find their life will lose it, and those who lose their life for my sake will find it." This is an invitation to selflessness, to patterning one's life on the life of Christ, who was so completely "for others."

In ordinary speech, "losing life" means physical death; in the vocabulary of spirituality, "losing life" paradoxically involves finding it. The believer participates in the riddle of the grain of wheat (John 12:24): "Unless a grain of wheat falls into the earth and dies, it remains just a single grain; but if it dies, it bears much fruit." This is just another way of saying that when we lose our old ways, we can enjoy abundant new life by engaging in any one of a wide variety of ministries, including hunger advocacy.

Lance Armstrong, cycling in 2001 to his third Tour de France victory, showed how good sportsmanship can demonstrate the truth of this "lose-your-life-in-order-to-find-your-life" philosophy. He put self-interest second to concern for his closest competitor, who accidentally rolled off the road and down an embankment. Neither biker nor bike was injured, so Armstrong slowed down and waited for his rival to catch up, and only then picked up speed and went on to win. This Scripture text is not a formula for doormat spirituality, but rather a prescription for Christian living.

Who better exemplified Christian living in our times than Mother Teresa of Calcutta? Listen to her words: "If sometimes our poor people have had to die of starvation, it is not because God didn't care for them, but because you and I didn't give, were not instruments of love in the hands of God, to give them that bread, to give them that clothing, because we did not recognize him, when once more Christ came in distressing disguise—in the hungry man, in the lonely man, in the homeless child, and seeking for shelter."[1]

---

1. Mother Teresa, *A Gift for God: Prayers and Meditations* (New York: Harper & Row, 1975) 24–25.

Christians committed to promoting the rights of poor people walk by faith, not by sight. It takes courageous faith to let your life fall, like a grain of wheat as if to die, into the soil of selflessness, confident that this "death," like the death of Christ, will bring forth fruit. "The death he died," Paul reminded the Romans (6:10-11), "he died to sin, once for all; but the life he lives, he lives to God." And so it is with committed Christian advocates, who, therefore, "must consider [themselves] dead to sin and alive to God in Christ Jesus" (v. 11). The question then becomes: What are we doing with those new lives? Advocates' answers to this question are written in words and deeds, large and small, in service to those who are powerless.

Children's Time [LH]

Giving our life to Jesus isn't something we do once in a while—it's an everyday thing. When we treat each other well, we show that Jesus is in our life. When we help someone in need, we're being like Jesus. When we decide not to do something that we know will hurt or make someone else unhappy, we're trying to be like Jesus. Try using seeds that you share with children to remind them that the seed changes as it grows. It becomes something very different, just as we do in gaining new shape and life.

Musical Suggestions [LH]

Brothers and Sisters of Mine Are the Hungry—BP 148

You Shall Cross the Barren Desert (Be Not Afraid)—BP 208

Never the Blade Shall Rise—GC 706

Blest Are You—GC 588

William J. Byron, S.J.

Thirteenth Sunday in Ordinary Time

RCL: Genesis 22:1-14; Psalm 13; Romans 6:12-23; Matthew 10:40-42

LM: 2 Kings 4:8-11, 14-16a; Psalm 89:2-3, 16-17, 18-19; Romans 6:3-4, 8-11; Matthew 10:37-42

"Here I am" is Abraham's posture before God. "Here I am" is what every believer hopes he or she will be able to say in response to God's call. That call is sometimes muted, usually nonverbal, typically persistent, and always awaiting a reply. "Here I am" begins the dialogue of faith and trust: "What would you have me do, Lord? What would you have me be or become?"

Is the "I am" in Abraham's response a biblical hint of the divine presence within each of us? We know that our God wishes to be known as "I AM" and instructs Moses to tell the Israelites, "I AM sent me to you" (Exod 3:14).

Like Moses and Abraham, each of us is in some way "sent." Yet we also must achieve within our hearts a radical freedom to be sent, to be responsive to whatever God asks of us. The story of Abraham being asked to sacrifice his son Isaac is a classic exposition of readiness before God, of responsiveness to God's will.

Another biblical hint lies hidden in this text—just a hint, but more, I think, than a pious imagining. "Abraham took the wood of the burnt offering and laid it on his son Isaac" (Gen 22:6). Read this against the background of John 19:16b-17: "So they took Jesus; and carrying the cross by himself, he went out to what is called The Place of the Skull,

134

which in Hebrew is called Golgotha." The Father's love for the Son along the Way of the Cross is interpreted for us in the love of Abraham for Isaac as they "walked on together" toward what might well have been Isaac's sacrificial death. God's will differed in these two instances, but the Father's love for the Son was just as firm in each case.

You might wonder about the conversation Isaac had with Abraham as they came down the mountain after sacrificing the ram instead of Isaac. "I told you that 'the Lord will provide,'" Abraham may well have said to his son. And you can only speculate on what version of a "sure-am-glad-he-did!" rejoinder Isaac may understandably have made.

To believe that "God himself will provide" is a test of faith for all believers who walk on an uphill journey against the odds. This is particularly true for those who believe that hunger can be ended and poverty overcome. God will provide. Experience teaches us, however, that God does not provide the meal, so to speak, nicely prepared and ready to eat. Nor does God provide a bank account to be drawn upon at will. God does provide human hands, hearts, and minds that can come to grips with what appear to be intractable problems. God does provide human commitment to work for change. God does provide a sense of justice. And God calls men and women to live their lives in generous service to others. So, like Abraham and Isaac, we "walk on together" knowing that "the Lord will provide."

Meanwhile, we know that "whoever gives even a cup of cold water to one of these little ones" can look forward to a reward. The Shunammite woman in the reading from 2 Kings also showed generous hospitality that led to joy and hope for her. Offering cups of water and showing hospitality are ways we welcome the outcast and stranger, the vulnerable and needy ones, and in turn are blessed. Even more important, we do what we can to apply intellect and political will to eradicate the causes of the poverty that is killing some and stunting the growth of others of our brothers and sisters in the human community.

Children's Time [LH]

Set a scenario for the children: When your mom or dad can't find you, they'll sometimes call out, "Where are you?" and you'll say, "Here I am." Many times in the Bible, when God speaks to people, they say, "Here I am." That doesn't mean "I'm over here," because God knows where we are; it means "I'm listening. You have my attention,

God." God is with us in many ways—when we pray, when we're scared, when we're happy, at our tables as we eat. In those special moments when God has something to say to us, we say, "Here I am."

Musical Suggestions [LH]

The First Song of Isaiah (Surely, it is God who saves me)—RSH 122

Lord God, Your Love Has Called Us Here—UMH 579

Jesu, Jesu, Fill Us with Your Love—PH 367

When the Poor Ones (Cuando el Pobre)—BP 154

Won't You Let Me Be Your Servant?—NCH 539

Where Cross the Crowded Ways of Life—LBW 429

William J. Byron, S.J.

Fourteenth Sunday in Ordinary Time

RCL: Genesis 24:34-38, 42-49, 58-67; Psalm 45:10-17 or Song of
Solomon 2:8-13; Romans 7:15-25a; Matthew 11:16-19, 25-30

LM: Zechariah 9:9-10; Psalm 145:1-2, 8-9, 10-11, 13-14; Romans 8:9,
11-13; Matthew 11:25-30

The words of Matthew 11:28-30 put an enormous responsibility on
the shoulders of the believer who is healthy, well off financially, intel-
lectually gifted, gainfully employed, and comfortably situated in life.
Presumably, these are not the people to whom Jesus is speaking when
he bids the weary and overburdened to come to him. But if those who
have wealth and influence do nothing to ease the burdens of the oppressed, the comforting words of Jesus become a mockery of those for
whom they were intended.

Consider the text: "Come to me, all you that are weary and are carrying heavy burdens, and I will give you rest. Take my yoke upon you,
and learn from me; for I am gentle and humble in heart, and you will
find rest for your souls. For my yoke is easy, and my burden is light"
(vv. 28-30). Easy? Light? Ask anyone who is poor and hungry if their
life is easy, if their burden is light. Ask yourself what they are likely to
make of this Gospel passage. Can they possibly believe it is intended
for them? Wouldn't we understand if they opt out, lose interest, and
choose a somewhat cynical self-exclusion from the benefits promised
in this optimistic message?

Unless you are content simply to blame the victim, you have to look around for what causes the physical and emotional weariness of those who suffer. You have to try to identify the source of the burdens that are crushing those who are powerless. If the causes remain unattended, the weariness will persist and the burdens will just grow heavier.

People living in poverty can't count on miracles. Hungry people cannot eat promises. Angels are unlikely to appear on the scene to ease their burdens. Humans helping humans is the way to make things happen, both because it is a realistic approach and because "miracles" can happen in communities of good and faithful people as long as they are patient and persistent.

Jesus offers a suggestion. "Take my yoke upon you, and learn from me," he says. Take upon yourself his yoke, not one of your own making. His yoke is always easy, unlike the ones we fashion for ourselves or heedlessly heap upon others. "Yoke" here refers to his interpretation of the law. We can learn from Jesus his law of love and see in his actions a demonstration of the truth that love consists of deeds, not words. Learning from him, we begin to wash each other's feet and carry one another's burdens.

We might even think of "yoke" as a verb and let ourselves be yoked to a law that is revolutionary and new. No longer content with a reciprocal "as-you-love-yourself" kind of loving relationship to neighbor, the new commandment calls for an ethic of renunciation, an "as-I-have-loved-you" sacrificial love that leads us to lay down our lives for another.

This Gospel is not calling for heroic, once-and-for-all sacrifice. It is a gentler call to day-by-day concern for easing the burdens of others. Where better to begin than by attending to hunger, the most urgent form of poverty? How better to address the challenge than by making a Bread-for-the-World kind of commitment to eliminating hunger through advocacy at those human, political decision points where those who are vulnerable and poor can be helped or hurt.

There was a wonderful Jesuit priest named Horace McKenna who was known as Washington, D.C.'s "Apostle to the Poor" when he died in 1982. He used to say that the Church without a social ministry would be like Christ without miracles. But, he added, "Our Lord did his miracles instantaneously at a word, but his Church, his brothers, his sisters, his fathers and mothers have to do their miracles slowly."

"Slow Miracles" is the name of the newsletter circulated by the combined soup kitchen and homeless shelter near the U.S. Capitol that bears his name.

Let this reflection close with one more saying repeated often by this saintly man: "I think we need to have marches—hunger marches, marches for the homeless, marches for peace. We need to make government realize that it should not spend our food money on armaments for war." St. Horace, pray for us!

Children's Time [LH]

Ask the children if they know what a yoke is. From a dictionary or other resource, show a picture of oxen or other animals with a yoke. It's heavy and is designed to make sure animals stay together and work together. Jesus says his yoke is "easy"! It's not a simple thing to follow Jesus, but what he means is that we are free to be his people and not be like others who have to put up with a heavier yoke. Jesus will help us be friends with him and with others, and he never gives us more than we can handle.

Musical Suggestions [LH]

Hope of the World—BP 176

Camina, Pueblo de Dios (Walk On, O People of God)—UMH 305

Lord of All Hopefulness—LBW 469

We Shall Rise Again—GC 772

Rev. Donald DiXon Williams

Fifteenth Sunday in Ordinary Time

RCL: Genesis 25:19-34; Psalm 119:105-112; Romans 8:1-11; Matthew
13:1-9, 18-23

LM: Isaiah 55:10-11; Psalm 65:10, 11, 12-13, 14; Romans 8:18-23;
Matthew 13:1-23 or 13:1-9

I have always been fascinated by identical twins because of their looks and the special bonds they are reputed to share. I grew up in an era when parents took great pride in dressing their twins in identical clothing. I am still in awe when I hear one twin finish the thoughts of the other. But these two characters in Genesis, Esau and Jacob, have forever altered my image of twins. This passage shows us twins who couldn't be more antithetical.

Before they are born, they struggle with one another in their mother Rebekah's womb. Esau becomes the cunning hunter who likes to be outdoors, while Jacob is the culinary artist who prefers to be indoors. Esau uses his brawn, and Jacob his brain. Their father Isaac loves Esau because he's a macho man, and Rebekah loves Jacob because he's a momma's boy. What really catches our attention in this text isn't so much Esau's willingness to use weapons to get food, but Jacob's willingness to use food as a weapon.

After a particularly grueling stint in the field, Esau comes home famished and wants to eat then and there. Borrowing Romans 8:5 terminology, Esau sets his mind on the things of the flesh (food) and does not attend to the things of the spirit (his birthright). He is desperate, and desperate people will do reckless things to satisfy a particular need. Jacob, in a less obvious way, is also desperate and is willing to use his food as a weapon to trick his brother out of his birthright.

Esau and Jacob's modern-day offspring are still struggling with one another. I cannot help but think of my brothers and sisters in Africa, who for years have been struggling with their siblings, on and off the continent. They struggled as victims of kidnaping. They struggled through the Middle Passage. They struggled as slaves on foreign shores. Now they struggle with hunger, poverty, AIDS, and wars.

The Genesis questions arise again. Are we rich nations collectively using food as a weapon against our kin? Are they willing to sell their birthright for a bowl of pottage? Are we coveting their gold, diamonds, oil, and other valuable birthrights, or will we find ways to help our brothers and sisters develop their land, bodies, minds, and spirits? When we free ourselves from the grasping spirit of Jacob, one day Africa will be able to do to us what Esau did to Jacob. Love us anyway.

Matthew 13 reflects Jesus' words as he explains the parable of the sower, talking about the seeds and where they are sown. Some seeds fall by the way; some seeds fall on stony ground; some seeds fall among thorns, and some seeds fall on good ground. Jesus equates the seeds with words of God's kingdom. As hunger advocates, we know the importance of seeds and of words.

Every morning as the escalator slowly brings me up from the below-ground Metro stop at Union Station in Washington, D.C., I see the very top of the U.S. Capitol and the surrounding area known as Capitol Hill. It has become my field of dreams for hungry and poor people. Our advocacy work for hungry people is much like sowing seeds. Just like winter, spring, summer, and fall, Congress has its seasons as well. This field has 535 acres: 435 members of the House and 100 senators. Our job is to sow seeds on each acre.

As in the parable, some of our words will fall by the way and die, never being heard. Some of our words will fall on stony ground. A legislator will gladly hear us, but when it comes time to vote for or cosponsor our bill or resolution, that congressperson, sometimes under pressure from others, will fall away. Some of our words will fall among the thorns. These are the ones who will hear our words and not like them. They will actively oppose the legislation, trying to kill it. Thank God, some of our words will fall on good ground and will yield good fruit, in the form of legislation that helps heal the nations. Therefore, when the congressional season is over, with God's help and after all our hard work of sowing, we will have a bumper crop for poor and hungry people all over the world. Sometimes your field of dreams can become a reality.

Children's Time [LH]

This week's parable of the sower, along with the story of the mustard seed in the weeks ahead, offers a chance to develop some seed-based themes, which have useful connections to hunger. Today you might bring in several containers with dirt, some with rocks clearly visible, some with weeds already grown up, some with rich, fertile soil. (If you've thought about this well in advance, you might even have planted some seeds so you can illustrate the result.) Ask which of these is likely to allow seeds to grow into strong and healthy and productive plants. Say that God wants our lives to flourish too and that God hopes we can receive the words God gives us in the Bible and use them as we love other people.

Musical Suggestions

Come, Ye Thankful People, Come—AAH 194

Brothers and Sisters of Mine Are the Hungry—BP 148

Rev. Donald DiXon Williams

Sixteenth Sunday in Ordinary Time

RCL: Genesis 28:10-19a; Psalm 139:1-12, 23-24; Romans 8:12-25;
Matthew 13:24-30, 36-43
LM: Wisdom 12:13, 16-19; Psalm 86:5-6, 9-10, 15-16; Romans 8:26-27;
Matthew 13:24-43 or 13:24-30

It is a good and wise thing to ask yourself the following questions
from time to time: What do I do? When do I do what I do? Where do
I do what I do? How do I do what I do? Who is with me when I do
what I do? And last but not least, why do I do what I do? In other
words, eventually we must ask, What is my motive?

I cannot speak for you but I can speak for me, so I'll bare just a little
bit of my soul. There have been times in my life when I have done the
right thing for the right reasons, done the wrong thing for the wrong
reasons, done the wrong thing for the right reasons, and done the
right thing for the wrong reasons.

I suspect that when it comes to personal or political things, other
people could say exactly what I've said. Every day advocates and legis-
lators for social change must struggle with the right and wrong of
issues as well as the motives behind the struggle. Politics can have a
funny way of messing with one's motives. Many decent people start
down the political road with good intentions, only to find out later the
unexpected place to which a well-paved road can sometimes lead. Yet
one's motives also can have a positive way of mediating one's politics.

143

Psalm 139 is a beautiful and powerful reminder that what we do, when we do, where we do, how we do, who we do, and why we do are monitored by the omnipotent, omnipresent, and omniscient God. I find it reassuring that through the messiness of the politics of war and peace; injustice and justice; poverty and wealth; racism, sexism, and classism; bad legislation and good legislation, God sees and knows every word and motive of every participant. We can have confidence that even in the hellishness of our personal, national, and international situations, God is somewhere above and within it all.

I like the imagery in Jacob's dream at Bethel in Genesis 28. A traffic jam of angels ascends and descends the ladder. God knows the who, what, when, where, how, and why of every angel on the ladder. This is good news for me because it frees me from worrying about others. I can concentrate on my own motives and say with the psalmist, "Search me, O God, and know my heart; test me and know my thoughts. See if there is any wicked way in me, and lead me in the way everlasting" (vv. 23-24). That is good advice personally, professionally, and politically.

For as long as I can remember, I have heard about mustard seeds. (Today the verses from Matthew that mention them are in the Lectionary for Mass readings and next week are in the Revised Common Lectionary readings.) I first found out about mustard seeds as a youngster in Sunday school, and I've heard more than my fair share of sermons over the years about having the faith of a grain of a mustard seed. However, I did not have my first direct experience with a mustard seed until 1998. Seeing and feeling it, rolling it between my thumb and finger, was fascinating. It was like meeting a biblical character in the flesh or perhaps meeting a long-lost relative for the first time. And the seeds are very small, just the way the Bible describes them.

The passage from Matthew 13 reminds me that many good things and ideas start out small. One such idea was the campaign called "Africa: Seeds of Hope" that Bread for the World sponsored as its Offering of Letters focus in 1998. The goal was to help small-scale farmers and rural communities in Africa by redirecting some of our nation's foreign aid resources. This would allow more African farmers (many of whom are women) to have the seeds, tools, small loans, and other things they need to help feed themselves and their families. Just like the tiny mustard seed, a small group of grassroots Bread for the

World members started writing letters, making phone calls, and visiting their members of Congress. What started out as something small ended with President Bill Clinton signing the Africa: Seeds of Hope Act into law.

There is a great song entitled "Ordinary People" I heard sung by Danniebelle Hall that says God uses ordinary people to do as God commands. The song's last line reminds us that when we put things in the Master's hands, God can make a little into a whole lot more. Truer words were never spoken.

Children's Time [LH]

Either this week or next, when you choose to use the mustard seed passage in Matthew, find some small seeds (ideally mustard seeds) and pass them out to the children. Tell the Bible story, focusing on how even small seeds can grow into larger plants and provide fruit, just as we can grow in our faith. Each of the children will get bigger as their bodies grow from the size they were as babies to adulthood; our prayer is that their faith will grow, too, as they trust and love God and love each other. You or your church's children's music coordinator could lead them in singing "We Are Climbing Jacob's Ladder," which offers a chance to sing and move around. While the theology of that image can be rather deep, it does show God's presence with us and care for us even in the hardest times of our lives.

Musical Suggestions

Lord, How Can We Feed a Hungry World? (Mustard Seed Faith)— BP 156

The Angels Keep A-Watchin'—AAH 130

We Are Climbing Jacob's Ladder—AAH 464

Order My Steps—AAH 333

Rev. Donald DiXon Williams

Seventeenth Sunday in Ordinary Time

RCL: Genesis 29:15-28; Psalm 105:1-11, 45b or Psalm 128;
    Romans 8:26-39; Matthew 13:31-33, 44-52

LM: 1 Kings 3:5, 7-12; Psalm 119:57, 72, 76-77, 127-128, 129-130;
    Romans 8:28-30; Matthew 13:44-52 or 13:44-46

Like the story of Samson and Delilah, this story in Genesis of Jacob, Rachel, Leah, and Laban has all the ingredients and intrigue of a first-rate made-for-television movie. As with any good soap opera, it has love, lust, sex, jealousy, sibling rivalry, deceit, and betrayal.

Because of his unsavory past, Jacob finds himself in a situation where he has to leave the comforts of his own home to find a new life in another place. He will be among people who are his family, but he does not know them and they do not know him. On his journey he meets his cousin Rachel, who tends her father's sheep. It's love at first sight, and soon he is in the home of his uncle, Laban. After a month Laban feels he should not let Jacob continue to work for him without some type of compensation. Jacob should have seen the movie *Jerry Maguire* and yelled like the Tom Cruise character, "Show me the money!" Instead, Jacob enters into a seven-year contract to work for Laban so that he can marry Rachel. Laban readily accepts the offer, and before you know it, the seven years are completed and Jacob is ready to marry and enjoy the company of the woman he loves. The only problem is that on his wedding night a switch is made, and the company he keeps is with Rachel's older sister Leah—the wrong one.

146

Jacob the trickster is tricked. If he wants Rachel, he now has to work another seven years, and he agrees. Now that's what I call love.

I told you this was sexy stuff! But now let's take a look at this story from another angle. In this version we see an immigrant going into a new socioeconomic environment, without a job or a place to stay or food, yet trying to find a better life. Like many other immigrants, he has family where he is going but doesn't know them very well. He ends up living in cramped quarters with his family and working in the family business for minimum wages, with long hours, poor working conditions, no benefits or Workers' Compensation. In the process of starting a family, he runs into unexpected problems that drain his already meager resources and keep him in his dead-end job twice as long as if he had labored under normal circumstances.

Many families today find themselves in situations very similar to Jacob's. Granted, people often contribute to their own problems, but there also are times when people find themselves dealing with situations and problems for which they are not responsible and over which they have no control.

That is why Bread for the World advocates for improvements in programs like Temporary Assistance for Needy Families (TANF). This assistance program can be the bridge to help low-income people bring their families out of poverty. Education and childcare can be very important tools to enable families to get and keep good-paying jobs that will help them leave poverty behind. BFW's advocacy helped more legal immigrants have access to TANF benefits. I wonder if Jacob would have qualified for TANF? He sure qualified for his own TV movie.

Some of the reasons that drive my vocation at Bread for the World today are found right in the passage from Romans. Long before I came to Bread for the World, Friday Morning Prayers, as we call them, were already engrained in the fabric of the movement. I am still impressed that every Friday without fail staff members in the BFW offices and others in the movement across the U.S. are praying. Many times after we have exhausted all our efforts and used all the tools of the trade of advocacy, we still need, and by God's grace have, the power of prayer. Verse 26 reminds us that even when we don't know what to pray for, the Spirit intercedes for us. With the power of the pen and the power of prayer, we have been able to move mountains and hills (Capitol Hill, that is). With confidence we can say that no matter how good or bad things look with the natural eye, in the Spirit "all things work together for good for those who love God, who are called according to his purpose" (v. 28).

Every time I read Romans 8:35, I remember a picture I saw in *Time* magazine showing a starving, weak, naked little boy struggling for his life, trying to make it to a nearby camp during the Ethiopian famine in the 1980s. Following him patiently is a vulture just waiting for him to drop. That image drives my work on the hunger issue today. I can only imagine what happened to that boy, but I know I love him and will never forget him. I feel confident that famine has not separated him from the love of God, which is in Christ Jesus.

Children's Time [LH]

You will want to resist the temptation to portray the soap opera aspects of the Jacob/Laban/Rachel intrigue. If you didn't do the mustard seed children's time suggestion last week, use that image or one of the other ones from the descriptions of the kingdom in this week's reading from Matthew. One idea is to bring in a piece of matzoh and a piece of regular bread, and point out that yeast makes the difference in the character of the two types of bread. (Make sure you're clear that matzoh is made for a special purpose and is not inferior because it lacks leaven.) How are our lives changed because God lovingly mixes leaven into our lives and causes us to grow in special ways?

Musical Suggestions

The Lord Hears the Cry of the Poor—BP 109

Guide Me, O Thou Great Jehovah—AAH 140

Kum Ba Yah—AAH 437

Jesus Loves the Little Children—AAH 616

Rev. Donald DiXon Williams

Eighteenth Sunday in Ordinary Time

RCL: Genesis 32:22-31; Psalm 17:1-7, 15; Romans 9:1-5; Matthew
14:13-21

LM: Isaiah 55:1-3; Psalm 145:8-9, 15-16, 17-18; Romans 8:35, 37-39;
Matthew 14:13-21

In the 1950s and early 1960s, my grandfather, Samuel Dixon, lived and worked as an engineer at the McReynolds Building, then located on the corner of 18th and G Streets, N.W., in Washington, D.C. Ironically, the building was just two blocks from the White House and directly across the street from the World Bank. Coming from my other grandfather's home, we drove past the U.S. Capitol building. These three places, then and now, represent in many ways three of the most powerful institutions in the world. But for a 10-year-old boy, they were just places I could ride my go-kart and play with my little brother. I knew that the president of the United States lived at the White House, and I knew that my grandmother worked in one of the Senate office buildings, but I didn't have a clue what was happening at the World Bank. In truth, I am still struggling to keep up with what is happening at the World Bank.

For all of their importance, none of these places was as important to me as the McReynolds Building. In that building, which housed apartments, Blackie's House of Beef restaurant, a barbershop, a grocery store, a shoe repair shop, a drugstore, and a diner, I learned about life, death, work, responsibility, and people.

I also didn't need any money at the McReynolds Building. One of this Sunday's verses, Isaiah 55:1, made me think of those days when I could go to that diner and Miss Edith or "Lil Bits" would fix me the biggest Cherry Coke at the fountain and the best cheeseburger in town. I could go to Mr. Morris at the grocery store, and he would give me anything I needed. I could go to Blackie's and get a steak that would melt in my mouth. Why? Because I was Sam Dixon's grandson, and in a day when segregation was the law, Sam seemed to be almost above the law, and in his own way he changed the law.

There is an old gospel song that says, "If it had not been for the Lord on my side, tell me where would I be, where would I be?" I can say the same thing about my grandfather. I don't know where or what I would be without him, but because of him and the good Lord and a few others, I am now in my own way trying to effect changes in those places near where I played as a child. Congress, the White House, and the World Bank have the capacity to help dig wells for clean water, provide debt relief for Heavily Indebted Poor Countries (HIPC), and provide aid and encourage trade that can improve the situations of people who don't have the resources to feed themselves.

My grandfather recently passed away at the age of 94 years young. I can't think of a better way to honor his memory than to try to help others as I saw him help others—and especially me.

I woke up the morning I started writing this reflection to the unexpected news that my cousin Bobby had died of an aneurysm and that his wake and funeral would be held in a few hours. Unlike my grandfather, who lived a good, long life, Bobby was cut off in the prime of his life. Still stunned, I jumped in my car, drove to the church, and paid my final respects.

Later that day, with Bobby still on my mind, I settled down to read the Scriptures for this reflection and received a wonderful gift. Matthew 14:13-21 is a tremendous example of Jesus using his personal pain to have compassion on others in the feeding of the five thousand. Jesus gets the news that his cousin John the Baptist has died of what I would call a man-made aneurysm. I imagine that many things were going on in Jesus' mind after getting this awful news. Should he stay and risk being killed himself, or should he run for his life? Should he keep a low profile and just drop out of sight, or should he lose himself in the crowd? Jesus chooses to do none of these things. He sees hurting people and heals them. He sees hungry people and feeds them. Other readings for this day, especially Isaiah 55 and Psalm 145, echo the bountiful, gracious way in which God feeds people.

In our lives as hunger activists, we are confronted with personal problems and situations that come into our lives. The events of 9-11-2001 brought this home to me. Thousands were suddenly cut off that day in the prime of their lives, including Odessa Lamb Morris, a childhood friend of mine killed at the Pentagon. We were shocked and hurt and still feel the personal pain of that day, but we know that there are hurting people who need healing and hungry people who need food. In verse 16 of the Gospel passage, Jesus says to us, "You give them something to eat." We have been called to work through our own pain to heal the hurt and hunger of others. With God as our helper, we will feed millions.

Children's Time [LH]

The story of the feeding of the five thousand calls for some creative action. Try arranging in advance with a couple of adults or older children to join the children during your time with them and to bring with them, concealed, some food to share. Take time to organize the children into groups, and after introducing the story, pull out what is an obviously inadequate amount of food—perhaps a cracker or two. As you mull this over, have the pre-enlisted other people, one by one and with growing excitement, offer to share what they have, making it a joyous (though not meal-destroying) feast. Remind the children that the miracle of this feeding story is that people took only what they needed to eat and that the situation encouraged all to share what they had because they had created community.

Musical Suggestions

I Saw the People Gathered—BP 151

Precious Memories—AAH 516, 517

Only What You Do for Christ Will Last—AAH 548

Rev. Donald DiXon Williams

Nineteenth Sunday in Ordinary Time

RCL: Genesis 37:1-4, 12-28; Psalm 105:1-6, 16-22, 45b;
Romans 10:5-15; Matthew 14:22-33

LM: 1 Kings 19:9a, 11-13a; Psalm 85:9, 10, 11-12, 13-14;
Romans 9:1-5; Matthew 14:22-33

Today's reading from Genesis brings up some strong emotions and memories I have not visited in quite some time. These verses made me reflect on some special people, special places, and a special purpose.

Joseph's story has great appeal to me on many levels. Joseph's big mouth, Isaac's favoritism, and his brothers' envy combine to set the stage for the revelation of God's ultimate purpose for their lives. In verses omitted from today's reading, it's clear that Joseph is the dreamer who does not mind telling his brothers about his dreams. Needless to say, his dreams do nothing to endear him to his brothers, because he is always the hero and they always come off looking subservient. Their hatred also stems from their knowing that their father loves Joseph more than he loves them. Sometimes before your dreams can come true and God finally and fully reveals God's purpose, you may just have to live through a nightmare. As the story unfolds, we see Joseph a captive of his own flesh and blood, put into a pit, sold into slavery, and taken to Egypt. Isn't it ironic, with all the joyous banquets in Scripture to which God invites us, that here the brothers sit down to eat in the midst of their brutal treatment of their younger brother.

Let me tell you how this story comes to life for me. In 1993 I went to Goree Island, off the coast of the West African country of Senegal.

In past centuries Goree was a center for the expanding European slave trade. Estimates are that well over 20 million Africans passed through the island. As I walked the paths on the island, I could feel the presence of those who went through the "Door of No Return." I found a rock that overlooked the island, sat down, and began to think about what it must have been like to be captured by your own people and put into the pit of slave dungeons and slave ships. What did they feel as they endured the "Middle Passage," then were sold as property into slavery, while their brothers and sisters were dispersed to South America, the Caribbean, and North America? As I sat there, tears came to my eyes, and I could feel my connection with Africa fill those empty places and penetrate the very viscera of my soul.

It is more than interesting to me the role that economics, money, greed, and hunger played in the enslavement both of Joseph and of those souls that were stolen away in the transatlantic slave trade. It is also inconceivable to me that at the dawn of the twenty-first century, slavery is still an issue in Sudan and in other parts of the world. It seems that economics, money, greed, and hunger are still at the root of our own inhumanity to one another.

Children's Time [LH]

This would be a classic time to speak with children about rivalries within families—that they exist and that most of the time we're able to cope with them by outgrowing them or working them out by talking to other family members about our feelings and needs. Obviously the Joseph story is a hard one, because today's reading ends without the more comforting resolution of next week's reconciliation. But either week offers a chance to acknowledge that tensions among brothers and sisters are often part of family life and to reject the violent, alienating responses of Joseph's brothers. Also be aware that part of what got Joseph in trouble was being seen as a tattletale, which children might wonder about.

Musical Suggestions

I've Been 'Buked—AAH 386

Oh, Lord Have Mercy—AAH 448

Rev. Donald DiXon Williams

Twentieth Sunday in Ordinary Time

RCL: Genesis 45:1-15; Psalm 133; Romans 11:1-2a, 29-32; Matthew 15:(10-20) 21-28

LM: Isaiah 56:1, 6-7; Psalm 67:2-3, 5, 6, 8; Romans 11:13-15, 29-32; Matthew 15:21-28

There is famine in the land. No matter how important you are or what position you hold in life, if you can't get food, eventually you will die. Given this pressing reality, the patriarch Jacob, hearing that there is grain in Egypt, unceremoniously tells his sons to get off their collective you-know-whats and go to Egypt to buy grain. When they arrive, Joseph immediately recognizes his brothers, but they do not recognize him. Time has a way of bringing about changes, and Joseph is no exception. When he left home, he was a wisecracking 17-year-old slave. Now he is a mature governor, full of wisdom. Only the king had more power. Isn't it wonderful to see how God has a way of making powerful those who are powerless? Just ask Nelson Mandela.

The passage from Genesis finds Joseph disclosing who he is but, more importantly, also expressing God's purpose in his suffering. Can you imagine what must be going on in his brothers' minds when they realize that the most powerful man in Egypt is actually the brother they sold into slavery? They are speechless to the point that Joseph has to tell them a second time who he is. He explains that God knew all along that there would be a famine in the land and merely used this situation as a vehicle to send him ahead to save their and others' lives.

In 1999 our plane touched down in Ghana in West Africa, and within hours Reverend Michael Thurman, my dear friend and pastor of the historic Dexter Avenue King Memorial Baptist Church in Montgomery, Alabama, and I were in a Sunday worship service at Calvary Methodist Church. Dexter Avenue and Calvary Methodist Church are sister churches, and Michael was guest preacher that Sunday. In the brief remarks I gave, I simply stressed the connection I felt as an African American with my brothers and sisters in the homeland and that although we'd been disconnected for hundreds of years, we are uniting again.

After the service two sisters, Mrs. Emma Kufi and Judge Helena Inkumsah-Abban, greeted us. Emma came with tears in her eyes and expressed her pleasure at having us return home. She said to us, "Your forefathers left these shores as slaves but have come back through you. You have not only survived in America but thrived in America, and now you are in a better position to help us." As she spoke, I reflected on this passage in Genesis. I could see Joseph and his brothers once again uniting with kisses and tears after a long and dreadful separation.

Take a moment right now and reread Psalm 133, savoring its rich images. It speaks volumes, my friends, about God's ultimate purpose.

Children's Time

[DDW] If you can arrange it in advance, invite children to bring in childhood pictures of their parents; put them on a board and have them guess whose parents they are. The point is to show how people change over the years, sometimes so much they're hard to recognize.

[LH] If you can't prepare in that way, remind the children about family reunions, or times when they've gone to see, or had visits from, family or friends they hadn't seen for a long time. Ask how they felt at those times, and share your own feelings about seeing people again after a long absence. Point out that people change over time and that sometimes it's important to put away old hurts, as Joseph did. What his brothers did to Joseph was terrible, but Joseph was later able to see that God took what had happened and made something good out of it, which allowed Joseph to greet his brothers and welcome them back.

Musical Suggestions

Unity—AAH 338

I Don't Feel No Ways Tired—AAH 414

He Brought Me Out—AAH 509

We Shall Overcome—AAH 542

Thuma Mina—AAH 564

Karen Fitzpatrick

■

Twenty-First Sunday in Ordinary Time

■

RCL: Exodus 1:8–2:10; Psalm 124; Romans 12:1-8; Matthew 16:13-20
LM: Isaiah 22:19-23; Psalm 138:1-2, 2-3, 6, 8; Romans 11:33-36;
    Matthew 16:13-20

"Who do you say I am?" It is startling when the preacher asks this question in worship, using the names of members present: "Jim Brown, who do *you* say I am?" Ask at least three members you know by name, both men and women.

We all need to respond to that question. The answers we give today are not the same ones that served us at age 10 or 20 or 35. Nor can our responses simply repeat what we have been taught, parroting someone else's answer.

Like Peter, I've learned from my heavenly Father who Jesus the Christ is for me. My life experiences are the means for this revealing. The gentle, loving Jesus of my childhood expanded as I matured, as I witnessed the Body of Christ suffering in places of war or famine. The bloated stomachs of kids with no future, the wailing of the relatives of those killed in Israel and Palestine, the silent witness of the mothers of the disappeared in Argentina—these have become the face of Christ to me. Dorothy Day challenging the war machine, Oscar Romero standing with his clergy and his people, Mother Teresa touching the disease-racked body of a dying man—these, too, are the face of Christ to me.

In Matthew's Gospel, Jesus asks his disciples about his identity at Caesarea Philippi. Visiting this lovely spot in northern Galilee today, the traveler finds cool and welcoming shade along the Banias River bringing water from Mount Hermon to the Jordan. In this place of quiet beauty and reflection, an answer can take shape. We, too, need a time to reflect on our experiences and identify their meaning, discovering Christ's presence in our midst.

The passage from Isaiah in the Lectionary for Mass describes the leadership the Lord desires, paralleling Peter's receiving the keys in today's Gospel. In Isaiah's account God approaches a worthy leader who will be the firm and well-fitted peg to support the tent in which God's people will dwell (v. 23). From this leader, Eliakim, we draw the "O" antiphon title for Christ, "O Key of David."

Perhaps our prayers in this Sunday's liturgy can reflect what we earnestly desire from our nation's leaders: the courage to open the treasury to help the poorest ones among us, to open the grain bins of our nation's Food Stamp Program to all who in justice would qualify. May God grant these same leaders the courage and firmness to shut down the flow of weapons to the world's poorest nations, weapons that ensure another generation of hungry children whose education is mortgaged to pay for arms.

The story of oppression and forced death of children in the reading from Exodus is replicated in our own time. It is relived as a mother walks miles to bring her sick child to the health clinic, only to discover the clinic has closed. Instead of supporting primary healthcare, government funds are allocated to repay the nation's debt, meaning that children will die needlessly from preventable diseases. It is repeated when a mother adds water to her infant formula to extend it and then sees her child waste and die rather than becoming fat-cheeked and healthy like the baby on the poster in the hospital.

Moses grew to health from his mother's own breast-feeding. Sadly, this natural and effective form of infant nutrition has faced denigration and lack of promotion as nations develop. Not just advertising, but policies and cultural norms get in the way of babies being fed in this way. Now, breast-feeding faces another threat with the possibility that HIV/AIDS can be transferred through breast milk. Present studies have mixed results. Confirmed studies show that breast-feeding not only passes on needed immunities and strengthens the mother-child bond but also provides enzymes needed for continuing brain tissue development.

Who do you say Jesus is?

Children's Time [LH]

Ask each child to say his or her name. Drawing on the Gospel story, remind the children that everyone knew Jesus' name, but Jesus asked his friends a harder question. His question—Who do you say that I am?—invited them to think about what Jesus really meant to them and to the world and to God. We are God's precious children, every one of us, so whether our name is John or Mary or Tamika or Ahmed, God loves us. That's who we are. Maybe someday when someone we don't know asks us who we are, we can say, "I'm someone whom God loves. My name is _____."

Musical Suggestions [LH]

Built on a Rock—LBW 365

Take My Life, and Let It Be—UMH 399

God Our Author and Creator—NCH 530

In Egypt under Pharaoh—NCH 574

Karen Fitzpatrick

Twenty-Second Sunday in Ordinary Time

RCL: Exodus 3:1-15; Psalm 105:1-6, 23-26, 45c; Romans 12:9-21;
Matthew 16:21-28

LM: Jeremiah 20:7-9; Psalm 63:2, 3-4, 5-6, 8-9; Romans 12:1-2;
Matthew 16:21-27

"Why are we so hated?" This was the common question after September 11, 2001. Those who see themselves as enemies of the U.S. are, in many cases, hungry or live in countries where the bulk of the population lives in poverty and often faces hunger. What are the connections between hunger and hatred?

Learning about our nation's foreign policy choices can offer clues. Does our country use food as a weapon or reward, or is food aid provided generously and impartially where there is need? How much foreign assistance is for development so that a poorer nation can become self-sufficient, and how much aid is for emergency relief? Or does it seem more intended to bolster U.S. economic interests? A cursory reading of the daily papers or a half-hour of headline news won't tell us all we need to know. It takes energy and commitment to be an informed citizen. United States citizens traveling in other countries are surprised at the depth and breadth of news coverage overseas compared with the froth we often are served. Some cope by subscribing to at least one periodical from the alternative press to get beyond the "company line" of the mainstream media, and some listen to public radio and the BBC.

We know the status quo can't continue. In today's reading from Matthew, Jesus calls us to self-denial, changing our own status quo. We who preach and lead congregations owe the people of faith no less than this: to be well informed, so that change can happen. If we know the scores and details of the sports world but are uninformed about global issues, a great possibility for some self-denial opens before us.

The reading from Romans spells out the unlimited parameters of that global concern. Feeding the enemy when they are hungry and giving drink when they are thirsty stretches us into a wider vision of community. Since famine hot spots change from year to year, a preacher attentive to global affairs will be able to pinpoint a current focus and help define a parish's response to hunger needs. Bread for the World's annual Hunger Report is a useful tool, and Bread for the World's Web site, www.bread.org, or toll-free number, 1-800-82-BREAD, offer updates on current legislation and hunger crises.

Responses to conflict and famine might include taking part in a denominational offering or organizing advocacy opportunities in the church. Calls or letters to Congress or the Administration could help enhance support for relief efforts or increase funding for development and self-sufficiency. But be aware: drawing from our Christian faith to love even our enemies can put us at odds with those who jump on the bandwagon of rampant nationalism and find any stance for peace-making unpatriotic.

Today's Gospel also speaks about gaining the whole world, which can lead easily into denouncing materialism and our modern obsession with possessions. A word of caution is in order. This is just too easy. We can send everyone home feeling guilty even about the roof over their heads.

Instead of dwelling in guilt, perhaps Francis of Assisi provides a model. He radically turned away from material possessions but took great delight in the material world with which God gifts us. Seeing creation as good is the first step toward responsible stewardship of this great earth. Naming objects as Brother and Sister, Francis showed his connection to the things of creation. His hymns of praise glorify God for all these material gifts. Yet Francis avoided attachment, never letting a thing achieve the importance that only another being or a relationship should have.

Both options for the first reading this week describe how God calls and sends. Jeremiah experiences God's name like a fire that he cannot hold in. We have all met people who are inflamed with passion for God and the things of God. We are in awe and wish for even a portion of the prophetic spirit.

But not too large a portion! I heard Megan McKenna speak on prophets a few years ago. For Judaism prophecy was a pillar, but in our Christian faith it is a very thin layer, McKenna said. Thus we often read the Gospels as emphasizing our individual relationship with Jesus rather than connecting us to a prophetic and covenantal tradition. McKenna said prophets care about the honor of God, the response to poor people's needs, and the coming of justice. And they are all one.

So we are called to be prophetic, not to be prophets of God's word, as was Jeremiah. We will all have our prophetic moments, but if we were to *be* a prophet, we would know it. We would have no other life.

Children's Time

From the reading from Romans find ways that children can bring food and drink to others. Use household examples, such as making a peanut butter and jelly sandwich for a younger sibling, turning on the drinking fountain for a smaller child at school, bringing a can of food for the church food collection, and taking part in the local congregation's hunger projects.

Musical Suggestions [LH]

Yigdal Elohim Chai (The God of Abraham Praise)—NCH 24

Now Let Us from This Table Rise—UMH 634

Make Me a Channel of Your Peace—FWS 2171

The Summons—FWS 2130

God It Was—GC 701

Karen Fitzpatrick

Twenty-Third Sunday in Ordinary Time

RCL: Exodus 12:1-14; Psalm 149; Romans 13:8-14; Matthew 18:15-20
LM: Ezekiel 33:7-9; Psalm 95:1-2, 6-7, 8-9; Romans 13:8-10;
Matthew 18:15-20

Treat the sinner in the church as you would a Gentile or a tax collector, Matthew's Gospel tells us. How are Gentiles and tax collectors treated in the Gospels and in the early Church? Gentiles are those outside the church community, but they also are the mission field. So now we're to expand this, making recalcitrant sinners part of the mission field, objects of preaching in the hope of converting their hearts. Tax collectors eat at Jesus' table. Do we need to work so sinners return to our tables of fellowship?

Even a confirmed sinner cannot be cast out without hope. Congregations throughout our country are split over the death penalty, despite pronouncements opposing it from many denominational leaders.

> We would regard it as barbarous and inhumane for a criminal who had tortured or maimed a victim to be tortured or maimed in return. Such a punishment might satisfy certain vindictive desires that we or the victim might feel, but the satisfaction of such desires is not and cannot be an objective of a humane and Christian approach to punishment.[1]

1. U.S. Catholic Bishops' Statement on Capital Punishment, November 1980; currently available online at http://www.osjspm.org/cappun.htm.

Today's Gospel invites challenging questions about where the call to reconciliation leads us. The passage from Romans, emphasizing loving neighbors as a summation of all the commandments, offers the same challenge. Reconciling with others and loving our neighbors lead naturally to a concern for whether they are fed and whether justice prevails in their lives.

Even for those who refuse reconciliation, we do not lose hope for future restoration. Prison chaplains tell us that movements like Kairos are able to help bring about true conversion of heart among the most hardened criminals in maximum and other high security prisons.

Frank was a real leader—in the wrong way. He was incarcerated at Lebanon Correctional Institution in Ohio, where Kairos was introduced as a weekend pilot project. The chaplain invited some leaders to attend, saying to Frank, "Give it a try. The worst thing that can happen is you waste a weekend."

"And it won't be my first wasted weekend," Frank commented as he agreed to attend. At the conclusion of the Kairos experience, Frank exclaimed, "The walls came tumblin' down! My parents, my wife, my children, my grandchildren couldn't bring down the walls, but tonight the walls came tumblin' down!"

A week later the director of food service, where Frank helped prepare the six thousand meals served each day, approached the chaplain, saying, "What did you do to my clerk? He's reading the Bible every day!" More than a decade later Frank continues praying. He has now moved to medium security.

Sister Helen Prejean has done more to focus national attention on the death penalty issue than any other individual. Long before the film version of her dynamic book *Dead Man Walking*,[2] Sister Prejean followed God's invitation that she write to a man on death row. A former English teacher then working in adult literacy among poor people in New Orleans, Sister Prejean tells how writing to the death row inmate led to a visit. Later she accompanied her first befriended inmate to his execution. Since then she has worked with several more death row prisoners and has become an international spokesperson against the death penalty.

---

2. Sister Helen Prejean, C.S.J., *Dead Man Walking* (New York: Random House, 1993).

The busy preacher needs both stories and facts. The Death Penalty Information Center offers many helpful facts through its website.[3] Their analysis shows that the U.S. is the only Western democracy with the death penalty and that our country leads the world in executing people for crimes they committed before the age of 18. The death penalty's deterrent effect is questionable, since murder rates in states that have abolished the death penalty are lower than states still using it. Too often innocent people are executed or are kept on death row but are later released because of new evidence of innocence. Racial inequities also characterize the way the death penalty is applied. Statistics show that cases involving life imprisonment are less costly to states than cases involving the death penalty.

Working for reconciliation is never easy, but it is also never optional in God's vision of a peaceful world.

Children's Time [LH]

Children may have profoundly negative images of people in prison, based on what they've seen or heard. They may think those in prison are bad people rather than people who have done some bad things. Perhaps someone in your congregation has worked as a tutor or chaplain in a prison setting and has seen and could tell about the kind of transformation that Karen describes above in Frank's life. Or you could use Frank as an illustration of how God breaks into our lives and cares for us, even when we resist and even when we've done some bad things. That's how deeply God loves all of us—even prison walls and bars can't keep God's love out of our lives.

Musical Suggestions [LH]

In the Midst of New Dimensions—NCH 391

The Gift of Love—UMH 408

As We Remember—GC 818

Lord of All Nations, Grant Me Grace—BP 178

---

3. The latest studies and statistics are available on www.deathpenaltyinfo.org.

Karen Fitzpatrick

Twenty-Fourth Sunday in Ordinary Time

RCL: Exodus 14:19-31; Psalm 114 or Exodus 15:1b-11, 20-21;
   Romans 14:1-12; Matthew 18:21-35
LM: Sirach 27:30–28:7; Psalm 103:1-2, 3-4, 9-10, 11-12;
   Romans 14:7-9; Matthew 18:21-35

Forgiveness. Even people of faith struggle to forgive when another's sin is terribly violent and obviously wrong, such as when it involves spousal or child abuse or murder of a loved one. "How could I forgive *that?*" the believer asks. "I could never say that was okay!"

This is when we need to clarify what forgiveness means.

Marie was moving along in the process preparing her for baptism at the Easter Vigil, when she and her two children would enter the waters of immersion into Christ. It was winter when the topic of forgiveness surfaced, and Marie sought me out for some private conversation. Her 9-year-old cousin had been murdered when visiting a friend overnight. The man who killed the two boys and the mother was apprehended. Adding salt to the wound, during the trial the perpetrator made a pass at Marie in the court hallway. He is now in prison. "I hate him with all my being," Marie said. "How could I ever forgive him for taking Jason's innocent life?"

Moving from such justified anger to the hope of forgiving is a long journey. It's a journey she needed to be on if she were to be baptized at Easter, for she could not be filled with hate and with Christ simultaneously.

My former parish colleague Martha Alken, O.P., has written a book called *The Healing Power of Forgiving.*[1] Her writing has helped me articulate to parishioners that their forgiving someone guilty of a heinous offense does not mean they're saying the act is okay. It means they will no longer let hate and unforgiveness be paramount in their lives. It means they are willing to recognize that the perpetrator is also a human being who is more than this one act. Once they allow the villain some humanity, then they can begin the process of forgiving.

Marie was not ready to forgive her cousin's killer by Easter, but she had resolved that she wanted to be able to forgive. She had begun the journey. We too can pray for the grace of a forgiving heart.

We can decide to walk in the spiral of forgiveness or in the spiral of violence. If we stand in the spiral of forgiveness, we choose nonviolent action in our relationships and in our approach to social issues. We will not bear a punishing attitude toward those receiving welfare assistance. We will support nonmilitary solutions to international conflicts, conscious of how entering the spiral of violence affects hungry peoples' lives and diverts resources from other social needs. We will support debt relief for the world's poorest countries so that they can rebuild their societies based on justice and wholeness. And we will forgive our political leaders when their voices and votes fall short of our hopes.

At times self-forgiveness is the most difficult gift to accept. John Shea, an author and storyteller, offers an intriguing interpretation of today's Gospel reading.[2] Pointing out the parallel phrasing in the two situations between the debtor and the king and then the debtor and the fellow servant, Shea suggests that the latter two may be the same person. The king forgives the servant, but the servant cannot forgive himself. This turns the second dialogue into a monologue. Being unable to accept forgiveness, he (and we) remain unforgiven.

You may disagree with Shea's view on this passage, but his perspective sheds fresh light on this story. When we cannot forgive ourselves, we tend to carry an attitude of unforgiveness into our relationships with others. We also get frustrated at our own responses to hunger and other problems, feeling we're never doing enough. Being gentle with

1. Martha Alken, O.P., *The Healing Power of Forgiving* (New York: Crossroad/ Herder & Herder, 1997).

2. John Shea, *The Our Father,* two audiotape cassettes, part 2, side B (Chicago: ACTA Publications, 1992).

ourselves and understanding that we can only do so much in the moments we have will let us persevere for the long haul. Since we don't work alone on hunger and justice advocacy issues but join many others in our witness to Congress, we can enjoy comfort and grace-filled rest rather than remain our own harshest critics.

Children's Time

Children often learn forgiveness at home in their early years as parents encourage them to forgive things their friends or siblings have done. Some of the best teaching of forgiveness for young ones, however, is when a significant adult models this by asking the child's forgiveness for a shortcoming such as impatience or inattention. Perhaps you could ask the children what it is like to be forgiven. When we give and receive forgiveness, we are building the reign of God—making the world more like what God intends.

Musical Suggestions [LH]

Where Charity and Love Prevail—NCH 396

Deep Down in My Soul—GC 880

Pues Si Vivimos (When We Are Living)—UMH 356

There's a Wideness in God's Mercy—PH 298

Karen Fitzpatrick

Twenty-Fifth Sunday in Ordinary Time

RCL: Exodus 16:2-15; Psalm 105:1-6, 37-45; Philippians 1:21-30;
Matthew 20:1-16

LM: Isaiah 55:6-9; Psalm 145:2-3, 8-9, 17-18; Philippians 1:20c-24, 27a;
Matthew 20:1-16a

Since the vineyard traditionally represents Israel and the harvest generally refers to the last judgment, the Matthean parable in today's Gospel is commonly interpreted that way. The "affirmative action employer" then represents God gifting everyone, even latecomers, with eternal life. So those of us who have been faithful for a lifetime would be hard-hearted indeed if we begrudge latecomers the gift of God's kingdom. Yet how human it is to do so. Who has not heard tongues of faithful churchgoers clucking about a "deathbed" conversion after a life of sin?

The parable also defends Jesus' outreach to marginalized people in Jewish society, in the face of complaints about his embracing tax collectors and sinners. Yet isn't this exactly the province of the Church's

169

ministry? Are we not called to embrace those on the margins of society in our time: immigrants; unemployed and underemployed people; those who are homeless, hungry, and destitute; gays and lesbians; unwed mothers; those with handicaps?

Scratching the surface of the Sunday congregation, negative attitudes can emerge toward one or more of the groups just mentioned. How might the preacher lay bare the prejudices that linger in the human heart despite all the human resource and church education programs that try to overcome them? How do we approach these attitudes (recognizing first that they exist in ourselves) and still preach good news? Probably by telling a story. At least that's what Jesus did.

The good news for this Sunday is God's generosity, so prodigious it is hard for us to comprehend, let alone imitate. In the Exodus story God offers quail and manna in quantities beyond what the Israelites can eat. They must learn not to overindulge, to take just enough for one day, to trust God's providence.

Bishop John McRaith of the Catholic diocese of Owensboro, Kentucky, illustrates this by pointing out that if we have three loaves of bread, normally we place one on our table, put one in the freezer for tomorrow, and give one to poor people. The challenge, he says, is to give away the second loaf. This takes us beyond generosity; it is trusting God to provide tomorrow's needs.

Our generosity should extend to the national levels as well. We in the United States like to think of ourselves as benefactors to the world, imagining that we are generous with our foreign aid. But surveys show that most people vastly overestimate how much our nation gives, thinking that about 20 percent of the federal budget goes to foreign aid, when in fact it is less than 1 percent.[1] Most citizens want to help needy countries and people but don't know how little we really do as a nation.

Our concern for justice compels us to look at today's Gospel reading without assuming that the vineyard owner is God. Although Matthew seems to lead us this way, the parable as Jesus may have told it is much richer and more engaging. *Parables as Subversive Speech* by William R. Herzog II offers a fresh look.[2] From Herzog we learn that

1. Bread for the World Institute, *Foreign Aid to End Hunger: Hunger 2001* (Washington, D.C.: Bread for the World Institute, 2001) 36–37.

2. William R. Herzog II, *Parables as Subversive Speech: Jesus as Pedagogue of the Oppressed* (Louisville: Westminster/John Knox Press, 1994) 79–97.

the day laborers of first-century Palestine were an expendable class who found work at planting and harvest time, begging or starving the rest of the year. In the story the owner makes a deal with those first hired (a denarius was an acceptable minimum wage for those in a sur-plus labor pool, but it was not enough to support a family). Later in the day the owner makes no pretense of setting a wage. Those workers will get what he determines to give them.

At the end of the day, when those who bore the day's heat have to watch others get their wages first, the owner shames them. As they raise a voice of protest, he singles one worker out as a spokesperson and makes a speech that he can do what he wants with his own money. Where is the biblical sense that the land is the Lord's and is given for everybody's use? Far from being a God-figure, the landowner shows the worst elements of an oppressive system. He tosses the spokes-person out of the vineyard. Now we see the workers' complaints in a new light.

What do people earn today working at jobs on the low end of our economic scale? We often hear that only teenagers hold minimum-wage jobs. Yet 40 percent of those earning the minimum wage in this country are heads of households; 68 percent are adults, age 20 and older. Congress has usually failed to raise the federal minimum wage regularly to at least keep up with inflation and lift families out of poverty. Advocates must continue to seek decent wages for working people.

How are hungry people experiencing the Lord's generosity through our nation's policies? How can we speak out on their behalf?

Children's Time [LH]

Bring three loaves of bread. Invite the children to think with you about how our families might decide what to do with those loaves. Eat one today, freeze one for later, and give one away for the church's monthly food offering might be a good approach. But then suggest to them what Bishop McRaith challenges us to do—to trust God so much that we'd consider giving away the second loaf, the one we'd freeze. Remind them of the Scriptures that discuss not worrying about tomorrow and how hard that is for us to do in today's world. Under-score that God certainly wants us to ensure that all are fed—and that's why we pay attention to that second loaf.

Musical Suggestions [LH]

All Who Hunger—FWS 2126

Lord, Whose Love Through Humble Service—UMH 581

Come, Labor On—NCH 532

All Who Love and Serve Your City—BP 165

Felipe Salinas

Twenty-Sixth Sunday in Ordinary Time

RCL: Exodus 17:1-7; Psalm 78:1-4, 12-16; Philippians 2:1-13;
Matthew 21:23-32

LM: Ezekiel 18:25-28; Psalm 25:4-5, 6-7, 8-9; Philippians 2:1-11 or
2:1-5; Matthew 21:28-32

To say that water is essential to life is so commonplace that we don't often stop to think about how many in our world today do without it. In fact, the chronic lack of access to clean water is a key cause of hunger. Without water for drinking and preparation of meals, for cultivation of crops, or for cleansing and medical use, people will experience hunger. No wonder, then, that we often use the language of "thirsting" to describe human attempts to fill emotional or spiritual longings. To experience thirst is to know that we need something or someone other than ourselves. In spiritual terms, genuine thirsting leads to faith and trust in God.

In today's reading from Exodus, the Israelites experience real physical thirst: they have no water and they vent their fears and anger against Moses. Their quarrel with Moses (and Moses' quarrel with God) translates the concern about physical thirst into spiritual terms. So after Moses produces water from the rock, the place of desert thirsting is transformed into Massah and Meribah, the place of quarreling and of testing God. Crisis brings the Israelites into a new place, where they ask a fundamental faith question: "Is the Lord in our midst or not?"

In a world where 1.1 billion people lack access to improved water sources,[1] while those of us in richer nations take access to water for granted, where are we to find modern-day Massah and Meribah? Certainly there are those who, in their physical thirst for water, have a right to quarrel and may even be forgiven for wanting to quarrel with God. But Massah and Meribah may well be located elsewhere, among those of us who question God's presence "in our midst," who lack faith in God. In that lack of faith we too often choose not to work to ensure that water is made to flow from our modern "rocks"—misguided spending priorities, ignorance of hunger's causes and solutions, and lack of political will.

For decades, hundreds of *colonias*—unincorporated Texas communities located along the U.S.-Mexico border—lacked basic water and wastewater systems. Residents were forced to truck in water from other sources and collect it from the scarce rain that occasionally falls in the area. Diseases such as tuberculosis, hepatitis, and dysentery became more commonplace. Beginning in the early 1980s, grassroots community organizations were formed through church communities under the umbrella of the Texas Industrial Areas Foundation Network. After years of leadership development of people with grade-school level of education, persistent advocacy, voter registration drives, and calling elected officials to accountability, results began to appear. By the late 1990s, through a combination of regulatory changes which ensure that future land developments include water and wastewater infrastructure, targeted state and federal funding, and local self-help initiatives, clean water started flowing into the homes of many of the nearly 500,000 *colonia* residents who continue to work for better living conditions.

The Scripture's quarrelsome mood continues in Matthew's Gospel, as religious leaders confront Jesus, intent on challenging the source of his authority. Like the Israelites in the desert, they, too, fail to see the Lord "in their midst." Jesus counters by asking their opinion of John's baptism: was it of human or divine origin? His questioners retreat, feeling caught between the two fears of hypocrisy and irrelevance.

---

1. See the United Nations website, www.wateryear2003.org.

Their lack of conviction is telling, especially in light of the parable of the two sons that follows. What matters in God's eyes is not words but actions. Because they are preoccupied with self-image, the leaders not only fail to act on their convictions, but they are effectively silenced.

How well do our professions of faith measure up with our actions, especially in God's vineyard, where the harvest of justice awaits? Do we find ourselves in a quarrelsome mood, raising objections born of political expediency, impracticalities, or comfort with the status quo? Or, perhaps worse, do we shrink from even daring to engage God's Word out of fear that our political convictions may be challenged and even changed?

Paul's grand hymn in Philippians tells how God's very nature is poured out in the Incarnation. In this ultimate act of humility, Paul sees the perfect model for Christians. Jesus "did not regard equality with God something to be grasped" (v. 6, New American Bible [NAB]). Even more so, then, we should set aside our quarrels with God—voiced or silent—and be willing to "empty" ourselves. Emptying ourselves leads us to thirst for justice that can become reality for all God's people.

Children's Time [MM]

As the children come forward, hold in your hand a tall glass of water, with ice, and perhaps lemon as well. Make it look attractive! As you recount the story of Massah and Meribah, take an occasional sip from the glass. Explain how easily the Israelites could have died in the wilderness without water. Remind the children that they can get a drink anytime they wish, while many children in the world don't get enough water or have to drink polluted water. Invite the children to thank God for the gift of water and for the gift of Jesus, who calls himself living water (John 4:10). Ask them also to pray that one day all the world's children will have fresh, clean water to drink. By now they might be getting thirsty! Someone might bring out a tray of cups with ice water as the children depart—for once, they may truly relish water!

Musical Suggestions [LH]

O Love, How Vast, How Flowing Free—NCH 209

Change Our Hearts—GC 394

Song of Hope (Canto de Esperanza)—FWS 2186

Felipe Salinas

Twenty-Seventh Sunday in Ordinary Time

RCL: Exodus 20:1-4, 7-9, 12-20; Psalm 19; Philippians 3:4b-14;
Matthew 21:33-46

LM: Isaiah 5:1-7; Psalm 80:9, 12, 13-14, 15-16, 19-20; Philippians
4:6-9; Matthew 21:33-43

It is hard to think of a biblical passage more well-known than the
Ten Commandments. They are so familiar that we run the risk of not
really allowing them to speak to us after repeated hearings. When we
consider fundamental readings like the Decalogue in the context of a
world that still hungers for bread and justice, clearly we must reexam-
ine and mine these readings once again. This passage is central in the
narrative establishing the covenant between God and Israel. For the
Israelites, the commandments gather together the core requirements
of their side of the covenant.

A common approach distinguishes the first four commandments as
focusing on the relationship of Israel to God, while the remaining six
treat matters dealing with relationships within the community. Before
Israel is admonished not to harbor false gods, they are reminded it is
the Lord, their God, "who brought you out of the land of Egypt, that
place of slavery" (v. 2, NAB) who is speaking to them. The context for
all that follows is this fundamental act of redemption, the Exodus.
Israel honors this redeeming God when it does not take God's name
in vain and when it keeps the Sabbath day holy. They do this not
simply because they are commanded to do so but because their relationship with God has been forged in the slavery endured in Egypt

and in their subsequent freedom, done through the hand of God and not through any actions of their own. The initiative has been God's all along. Their worship should be an expression of gratitude and deepening intimacy. But their intimacy with God cannot be divorced from their relationship with one another, for the remaining commandments demonstrate what follows from a covenant relationship with God. If they are to be partners with God in this covenant, they are not to kill, to testify falsely, or to covet what others have. Doing any of these things not only destroys their human community but also breaks the covenant with God.

What do the commandments mean to us in a world where so many still lack food, clean water, and access to healthcare and basic education? Especially in view of the even more direct way in which Jesus connects love of God and love of neighbor, isn't our fundamental relationship with God compromised—rendered less than it should be—as long as we allow such fundamental affronts to basic justice to persist?

When our son Ben was in his early teens, he became intrigued by Heifer International, which provides farm animals to poor families around the world. These animals not only produce milk or eggs, but their offspring also are shared with neighbors to promote ongoing community development. As we approached the Christmas season, Ben decided to organize a family contribution to buy an animal for a Heifer International community, encouraging us all to remember others at that time of year. Ben e-mailed his uncles, aunts, and cousins with his plan, and on Christmas Day, at our family gathering, he proudly announced that they'd raised nearly $100 and that the contribution would soon be on its way! Ben's effort reminded us that our prosperity and life are gifts we must use for others who still lack life's basic necessities, connecting love of God and love of neighbor.

The parable of the Wicked Tenants in Matthew's Gospel concludes an exchange between Jesus and Jerusalem's religious leaders concerning the source of his authority. Jesus' point in the parable is that it doesn't matter what you profess to believe if your actions don't conform to those stated beliefs. The issue is faithful stewardship: how do we use what God has entrusted to our care? Perhaps we need to take inventory; do we even recognize that what we think is "ours" really belongs to God? The chief priests and Pharisees realize that the parable is about them. Their response is to lie in wait, fearing the crowds that regard Jesus as a prophet.

Are we like these fearful leaders? How receptive are we to God's Word? Are we open to hearing the challenge to live faithfully, or do we instead choose self-interest and personal gain? Being a faithful tenant means recognizing our utter dependency on God's grace for all that we have and are. More than that, it also requires that we not squander the gifts we've been given, because, ultimately, God's gifts are to be given away in the service of God's people, especially those who are most vulnerable.

Children's Time [MM]

Explain to the children about the Ten Commandments—how the first four pertain to our relationship with God and the other six to our relationship with one another. You might even write these out on "tablets," with these headings: "Getting along with God" and "Getting along with others." Think through the "Getting along with others" tablet with them. What happens if we respect our parents? What if we don't? What happens if we steal, kill, envy, lie? What if we don't? It's all about living in peace with one another.

Ask what happens if people don't have enough food. Is there more of a chance that they might lie or steal if they're hungry or they have family members who are hungry? Fighting hunger and working for justice are keys to getting along with others. Remember, too, that getting along with God helps us in getting along with others. Through Jesus, God always gets along with us, even when we don't hold up our end of the relationship!

Musical Suggestions [LH]

God of Abraham and Sarah—NCH 20

Christ Is Made the Sure Foundation—GC 662

O Christ, the Great Foundation—NCH 387

How Clear Is Our Vocation, Lord—PH 419

Walter Wink

Twenty-Eighth Sunday in Ordinary Time

RCL: Exodus 32:1-14; Psalm 106:1-6, 19-23; Philippians 4:1-9; Matthew 22:1-14

LM: Isaiah 25:6-10a; Psalm 23:1-3a, 3b-4, 5, 6; Philippians 4:12-14, 19-20; Matthew 22:1-14 or 22:1-10

> [**Note:** Walter Wink's reflections for this week through Christ the King Sunday focus exclusively on the Gospel passages for these weeks.]

There are three extant versions of this Gospel parable of the Wedding Banquet. Matthew's is clearly the most modified. Neither Luke 14:16-24 nor the Gospel of Thomas (henceforth GT) 64:1 knows anything about a king giving a marriage feast. Luke treats it as a great banquet, and GT as merely the meal required to feed visitors. Luke and GT depict the invited guests as making flimsy excuses to jilt the host, whereas Matthew slights the excuses and in their place spins an allegory in which the king's subjects not only refuse to come when invited but also kill the servants sent to invite them. In verse 7 Matthew abandons the guise of allegory for a straight-out historical allusion to the destruction of Jerusalem in the Jewish War of 66 C.E. Obviously, Jesus couldn't have spoken these words some 40 to 60 years after his death!

Matthew then adds a brief warning to wear the requisite wedding garment, and the punishments in store for those who do not. Here we encounter Matthew's signature warnings: "cast him into the outer darkness, where there will be weeping and gnashing of teeth" (v. 13). Luke and GT know nothing of this threat. Almost all the references to eternal fires, torments, and tortures in the afterlife appear in Matthew's Gospel, and often when Matthew mentions them, Mark, Luke, and GT do not. So Matthew's version appears to be furthest from the original.

But Luke also has a few elements that don't suggest early tradition. Verses 21b-23a seem repetitious and added to provide an allusion to the Gentile mission. As such it is redundant. If we set aside those verses, we have something pretty close to what may have been the original.

GT is preoccupied with the excuses, which he makes more elaborate and refined. Consistent with that interest, GT has added a fourth excuse. Those who jilt the host are in every case wealthy men of great importance. Their refusal to attend would have been a deliberate act of humiliation. The host would have to have done something serious to warrant such treatment. GT ends the parable with a didactic slam: "Buyers and merchants will not enter the places of my Father."

So the odds are that the Lukan version is the most original, minus the verses indicated. But what is the point?

Matthew explicitly states that this is a parable of the reign of God. But what is that reign? It is a new order of power that turns the pyramid of power upside down. That paradox is revealed here as God having a preferential option for those who are unemployed, hungry, destitute, and marginal. To quote Luke precisely, these are "the poor, the crippled, the blind, and the lame" (v. 21), a phrase Luke himself has added to make clear who can come to the dinner.

In societies like first-century Palestine, there was a very flimsy safety net, made up mostly of alms that were inadequate to provide enough calories for one person, much less a family. People literally died on the streets (Luke's story of Lazarus and the rich man in 16:19-31 is a case in point). The unemployed dropped through the copious rips in the net, and many would rapidly succumb to starvation and its related diseases.

It is these, the hungry people, who are invited to the feast. Metaphorically, that feast is the presence and coming of God into this world. But metaphorical feasts are never satisfying unless everyone is fed at a literal feast. Jesus is saying that there is abundance if only it is shared. Shockingly, there are many who will have nothing to do with this feast and refuse to attend. There is food enough for all, but not the will to share. Bread for the World's mission is to see that the bread is shared. In the face of widespread starvation, hunger, and homelessness even in the developed nations, we must be careful to see that the literal feast precedes the figurative feast.

More personally, we might make a list of excuses that keep us from feasting. On one side, ask yourself, "What are the preoccupations that so fill my life that I have no time for the feast?" On the other side, "What is the poverty, brokenness, or infirmity by virtue of which I may be brought to the feast?"

Children's Time [LH]

Ask the children how many have ever gone to a meal where there were lots of people present. These may have been family picnics, wedding receptions, birthday parties, or other events. We often call these feasts, and they're a time for celebration and rejoicing. Sometimes when we're invited to a feast we have to say no because we already have other plans. But in our story today, we're reminded that God welcomes all of us, whether we're poor or rich, young or old, to the wonderful feast God has ready for us. And like God, we're also to welcome others to share food around our own tables so that all God's people can be fed, each day. What a joyous feast!

Musical Suggestions [LH]

Lord of Feasting and of Hunger—BP 141

Now the Feast and Celebration—GC 742

As We Gather at Your Table—FWS 2268

Now We Join in Celebration—LBW 203

You Satisfy the Hungry Heart—PH 521

Praise and Thanksgiving—GC 764

Walter Wink

※

Twenty-Ninth Sunday in Ordinary Time

※

RCL: Exodus 33:12-23; Psalm 99; 1 Thessalonians 1:1-10; Matthew
  22:15-22
LM: Isaiah 45:1, 4-6; Psalm 96:1, 3, 4-5, 7-8, 9-10; 1 Thessalonians
  1:1-5b; Matthew 22:15-21

This passage from Matthew about paying taxes to Caesar is confus-
ing. Does it mean that there are two realms of reality—one presided
over by the prince (president, prime minister, magistrate, etc.), the
other by the bishop (presbyter, pastor, preacher)? This is the all too
familiar "two realms" theology of the period before World War II.
That theology underwent devastating criticism due to the way the
"German Christians" co-opted it, being willing to tolerate Nazism as
long as it didn't encroach on the realm of the church. "Give therefore
to the emperor the things that are the emperor's, and to God the
things that are God's" (v. 21) appears to say that payment of tribute is
a secular matter, and that Jews must pay it because it belongs to "the
emperor." According to this interpretation, tax resistance such as the
early American colonists or opponents of the Vietnam War engaged in
would be a violation of the neat distinction between the two realms.

Most interpreters have rejected the idea that there could be any
reality at all that is not subject to the sovereignty of God. Besides,
Jesus is not talking in the abstract about political science; he is talking
about the Roman emperor, and not about just any taxes, but the
galling tribute extorted at sword point from a subjugated people.

There were few Jews who would concede that the emperor was legitimately sovereign over anything. The Jews who no longer could stand Roman misrule of Palestine and who rebelled in 66 C.E. would not concede an ounce of Jewish soil. So Jesus comes dangerously close to betraying Jewish sentiments when he concedes anything at all to the emperor.

But we need to look more closely at the context. Jesus is not just any place; he is in the Temple of Jerusalem, the major employer in all Palestine, an institution so corrupt that the Essenes withdrew to the desert in protest against a high priesthood that the Romans sold to the highest bidder. Jesus is standing, then, in what he calls "a den of robbers," Israel's holiest institution, now sunk so low that the powerful clique of urban priests used gangs of thugs to bully rural priests out of their fair share of Temple proceeds, leaving them destitute.

It is people of that ilk who attempt to trip Jesus up. Their trap is cleverly set. If Jesus says pay the tribute, he risks alienating the very people on whom his success depends; if he says no, he risks his very life, since to speak thus would be treason.

Jesus asks for a coin. They hand him a denarius. This is not the Tyrian coin used in the Temple, but a Roman coin used to pay the legions in the eastern part of the empire. It bore the image of the emperor on one side and a god on the other. The inscription read, "Tiberius Caesar, Son of the Divine Augustus." Every Jew had to pay Rome tribute, payable at one denarius per head. Simply to have such a coin in one's possession in the Temple was a shocking concession to Roman paganism. "Whose head is this, and whose title?" (v. 20). Caesar's. Well, then, since you yourselves have already conceded Roman authority over you, go on, pay tribute, since your souls already have Caesar's image stamped upon them. But if your souls had the image of God stamped upon them, you would not yield to idolatry and tolerate the image of Caesar in the Temple. After all, Caesar had already been granted the status of son of the god Augustus.

Jesus, in short, hands them not an explanation but a conundrum. His only chance is to answer so elliptically that no one can be sure where he stands. But his ruse doesn't work. We at least know how some of Jesus' opponents understood him. In Luke 23:2 one of the charges made against Jesus is "forbidding us to pay taxes [tribute] to the emperor," a charge too dangerous to have been invented by the Church.

As José Cárdenas Pallares puts it, if God is the absolute, and the emperor is not God, then we cannot put God and Caesar on the same level. "My obligations to Caesar, if any, must be judged by the yardstick of my commitment to God."[1] Therefore, whatever infringes on God's sovereignty must be resisted by every means consistent with the new reality that Jesus reveals.

Children's Time [LH]

Since a coin with Caesar's image on it plays such an important role in this story, it's probably a good idea to show one of our own U.S. coins and note that a president's head is on it (a quarter might be the most recognizable to children). Remind them that the Roman emperor had a very different status than the U.S. president: we admire but don't worship our presidents.

In the times when Jesus lived, many people saw the Roman emperor as a god, but that's not who the people who followed Jesus and the Jewish people in Israel worshiped. They worshiped the God we know in the Bible. In our daily lives, that is the God we worship too. We use our money to pay our bills and support the church's work, but we don't worship our money or the people whose pictures are on it. God is the one who hears our prayers, takes care of us, and loves us.

Musical Suggestions [LH]

Take My Life—PH 391

O Young and Fearless Prophet—UMH 444

O God of Earth and Altar—NCH 582

Take My Gifts—NCH 562

---

1. José Cárdenas Pallares, *A Poor Man Called Jesus: Reflections on the Gospel of Mark* (Maryknoll, N.Y.: Orbis Books, 1986) 76.

Walter Wink

Thirtieth Sunday in Ordinary Time

RCL: Deuteronomy 34:1-12; Psalm 90:1-6, 13-17; 1 Thessalonians
2:1-8; Matthew 22:34-46

LM: Exodus 22:20-26; Psalm 18:2-3, 3-4, 47, 51; 1 Thessalonians
1:5c-10; Matthew 22:34-40

There are three different versions of the Great Commandment story.
In Matthew and in Mark 12:28-34, Jesus answers; in Luke 10:25-28,
the lawyer does. Which seems more probable: that Jesus articulated
this splendid summation of the law, and then Luke placed it on the lips
of one of Jesus' opponents, or that a Jewish lawyer originally said it
and someone in Christian circles awarded it to Jesus? My guess would
be the second.

Another difference: in Matthew and Mark, the issue is summarizing
the law, whereas Luke changes the issue to "What must I do to inherit
eternal life?" (v. 25). Again, which is more likely: that the original
question was about the law or about eternal life? My guess, again,
would be the second. Luke is writing primarily to Gentiles, for whom
the issue of the law would be irrelevant. So Luke borrows the question
asked by the rich young man (Luke 18:18) and brings it here. This is a
beautiful example of how the tradition must be continually modified
to speak to new generations from different cultures. Fundamentalism
is the refusal to make such modifications. It freezes the tradition, so
that modern people are forced to make a sacrifice of their intellects and
hold on to the old tradition unmodified. Luke has not falsified the
tradition by changing it; that is the only effective way to live it forward
in a new time and place.

In Matthew and Mark, Jesus answers the question about the summation of the law by first citing the Shema, Israel's basic affirmation (Deut 6:4-5): "Hear, O Israel: the Lord our God, the Lord is one; you shall love the Lord your God with all your heart, and with all your soul, and with all your mind (Mark adds 'strength')." He then adds a passage from Leviticus 19:18: "You shall love your neighbor as yourself." Together we have a perfect match—love of God, love of neighbor.

Curiously, in many churches this "double love commandment" is repeated as a part of *Christian* liturgy, and most Christians regard it as unique to Christianity. But as we see above, in all likelihood the lawyer, not Jesus, first articulated this coupling. This statement in fact is the essence of Judaism! How many times have we heard (and even repeated) the old saw that Judaism is a religion of wrath, Christianity a religion of love. But this is a thoroughly *Jewish* affirmation. And in some tragic cases, Christianity has proven to be the religion of wrath, violence, and domination. When it comes to love, Christians have lots of work to do.

This summary of the law has often been characterized as the "double love commandment." But that is inaccurate. It is the *triple* love commandment: love God, your neighbor, and yourself. Many Christians have heard that, unfortunately, as "instead of yourself." But Jewish tradition is adamant here. You cannot love your neighbor unless you love yourself. This is, in fact, the only commandment that Christians have always obeyed: you always love your neighbor as yourself. You can only love others to the degree that you love yourself. If you hate yourself, you will hate others. Perhaps that is why the love of God must precede the love of neighbor and self, for our own lovelessness needs the therapeutic touch of divine love in order to be healed and our hearts opened to love ourselves and others.

The second passage in today's Gospel selection is the dispute about David's son. This is one of the most mysterious passages in the New Testament. This passage seems to assert that Jesus is not the Messiah. As Herman Waetjen puts it, "David's lord is none other than the New Human Being [son of man] whom Jesus embodies and manifests . . . who, because he is David's lord, cannot be David's son" (Matt 22:41-46).[1]

---

1. Herman Waetjen, *A Reordering of Power: A Socio-Political Reading of Mark's Gospel* (Minneapolis: Fortress Press, 1989) 195.

Jesus repudiated the Davidic or messianic role, dripping as it was with violence and domination, and replaced it with "the son of the man" (which is ascribed to Jesus over 80 times). He almost never identifies himself with the Messiah, and these few instances may have been inserted by the Church. In place of the supreme commander of the armies of God and man, Jesus saw himself as powerless, nonviolent, compassionate, and lowly—a nobody exalted to God, as this passage attests.

[Editor's note: For Roman Catholic parishes, today's reading from Exodus 22 contains important language relating to not oppressing aliens and avoiding exploitation in economic relations. These may present good opportunities for homilies in your setting and ministries, particularly if your parish has been active in advocacy in the Jubilee 2000 movement or in working to restore food stamp, TANF, and other federal benefits to legal immigrants.]

Children's Time [LH]

Depending on the age of the children involved, it might be tricky to try to talk about loving yourself, though esteem and self-care issues can be very real for young people of certain ages. A more conventional approach would be to talk about loving God and neighbor—and to emphasize the inclusiveness of the term "neighbor." It's helpful to remind them that because of TV, computers, and other means, we know much more about people far away and how close we are to them. Perhaps bring pictures of children from other countries or other parts of our own nation. Ask them if they know people who live far away and how they consider them neighbors despite the distance. We can love them just as we can love those who live right next door.

Musical Suggestions [LH]

O God of Love, O God of Peace—PH 295

The Gift of Love—UMH 408

Un mandamiento nuevo—NCH 389

Spirit of God, Descend upon My Heart—NCH 290

Walter Wink

Thirty-First Sunday in Ordinary Time

RCL: Joshua 3:7-17; Psalm 107:1-7, 33-37; 1 Thessalonians 2:9-13;
Matthew 23:1-12

LM: Malachi 1:14b–2:2b, 8-10; Psalm 131:1, 2, 3; 1 Thessalonians
2:7b-9, 13; Matthew 23:1-12

Much of the intolerance and hatred directed toward persons of other
religions arises from the failure to recognize religion's inescapable
ambivalence. Religion is the source of our highest values, role models,
love of creation, self-sacrifice, consolation, outrage against injustice,
and much more. But religion also generates prejudice, exclusion,
witch hunts, crusades, inquisitions, patriarchal dominance, the abuse
of children, fanaticism, holy wars, and the murderous conviction that
we alone are right. All religions are guilty of these aberrations, without
exception.

To be sure, the great religions are paths to the divine. They have
produced saints, mystics, wise women and men, great teachers of the
religious path. But typically only one side of the ambivalence is acknowledged. Adherents of religion A condemn religion B for not
living up to the highest values of religion A; meanwhile, adherents of
religion B condemn religion A for the same. And the criticisms of both
may hold some truth.

This is the necessary background for reading Matthew 23. Most
members of the early churches were Jews, and so their controversy
with other Jews was an in-house dispute between coreligionists. The
scathing attack on the scribes and Pharisees here has not yet com-

pletely degenerated to name-calling and rejection. For Matthew makes it clear that the disciples of Jesus are to *obey* the Jewish religious authorities. Considering later hatred between Christians and Jews, this willingness to stand under their opponent's authority is amazing.

Both parties make serious charges, worded with biting force. But the author of Matthew's Gospel makes this qualification: Do what they say, but not what they do. At this point the disputants still honor the ambivalence of the religion over which they quarrel. Would that later Christians had maintained the distinction! For this holds as a critique of all religions: Do as they say, but not as they do.

And what are the charges Matthew's synagogue brings against its rivals, ostensibly in other synagogues? First, that they burden people with laws and customs that take all the joy out of religion, smear them with guilt, and bring them under the authority of people for whom they have no respect and who only say but don't do. Pause there. Do we for one moment think that Matthew's community was not guilty of the same behavior? "They do all their deeds to be seen by others" (v. 5). Do Christians not do the same? Of course they try not to do so, but they lapse. Egos get in the way. People want to be well thought of, so they fall into the very trap their opponents have. Both sides claim the other says but doesn't do.

The same goes for Matthew's other charges. The scribes and Pharisees dress with religious ostentation. They jostle to get the most prestigious seats in the synagogues and love to be loudly acclaimed as religious leaders in public places. Do we think that Christians do not do the same? How else do we explain the regression in the early Church to patriarchal power arrangements that excluded women from power and office and created new offices far more dictatorial than anything in the synagogues (which were much more democratic) and liturgical garb far more ostentatious than their Jewish neighbors?

Jesus tried to head this off. He forbade titles like rabbi, teacher, or master, claiming all such honors for God, who alone is our Rabbi, Teacher, and Father. No titles, no Ph.D., D.Min., no M.D., no M.S.W.—none of that trash, because Jesus demands equality, and titles create hierarchies that inevitably exclude, shame, and treat others as inferiors. Instead, he provides a standard of behavior in which the powerful renounce prestige. The greatest is a servant. The world had never seen such an inversion of power—and in most churches, it still hasn't.

Children's Time [LH]

Today's lessons offer at least two good opportunities. One is to underscore the difference between saying and doing arising in the Gospel story. Some examples of "saying" that children understand are when they say they'll keep their room clean, or remember to put their bike away, or come inside from playing at a certain time, or be nice to a friend or neighbor. Adults have their own things like that—mention a few of your own, including some serious ones like praying. Sometimes we really mean to do those things, but we don't actually do them, or we do them only part way and expect to get all the credit. Because we love God and God loves us, we make promises to God, such as loving each other and helping those who are in need. God wants us not just to say those things but to do them with a glad heart.

A different possibility for children's time arises from Psalm 107:35-37. Bring in a large bowl or box filled with sand and have children run their hands through it. Read the psalm text from a popular translation, as it speaks of God making things grow in the desert. We think of sand when we think of the beach or a sandbox to play in, but a sandy desert is not a place we think of for growing things, where people can live and eat enough. But God can do many things, bringing life to places where there isn't any, giving us hope when we're sad, offering food to everyone who is hungry. God can do amazing things, and we can help do God's work.

Musical Suggestions [LH]

Jesu, Jesu—UMH 432

Together We Serve—FWS 2175

Won't You Let Me Be Your Servant?—NCH 539

O Praise the Gracious Power—PH 471

Walter Wink

⬛

Thirty-Second Sunday in Ordinary Time

⬛

RCL: Joshua 24:1-3a, 14-25; Psalm 78:1-7; 1 Thessalonians 4:13-18;
Matthew 25:1-13

LM: Wisdom 6:12-16; Psalm 63:2, 3-4, 5-6, 7-8; 1 Thessalonians 4:13-18
or 4:13-14; Matthew 25:1-13

Palestinian weddings were the most cherished celebrations in an otherwise dreary regimen of exhausting work. Men engaged in foot-races, camel or ass races, games of skill, and drinking. Then the bride-groom, after payment of the bride price to his in-laws at his father's house, would lead a nocturnal, torch-lit procession in the company of his friends to claim his bride at her father's house. Female friends of the bride awaited the groom's coming and would go forth to meet him, bearing, according to custom, olive oil lamps held aloft on poles. At this juncture the bride would join the swelling procession, which would journey the distance back to the bridegroom's own home for the wedding feast. The hour of the bridegroom's coming, however, could not be predicted. If the legal proceedings were protracted, he might arrive extremely late at night. On occasions when the groom was delayed for this reason or when the distance to his home was con-siderable, the wedding feast was celebrated at the bride's home.

It was the task of the unmarried females to illuminate the wedding feast. "Virgins" here are simply unmarried young girls, who were typi-cally married at around 12 years of age. It is plausible that the foolish young maidens could still purchase oil at midnight, since everyone in the village would be waiting for the groom to come.

This parable has frequently been treated as a Christian allegory of the marriage of Christ and his Church. But the bride never makes an appearance. The meaning, then, must be sought in the ten maidens, not the bride and groom.

The theme of watchfulness, which is introduced in verse 13, is at odds with everything in the parable and is clearly a Matthean insertion (Matt 24:42, 44, 50). The parable doesn't distinguish between those who sleep and those who keep watch; all the bridesmaids sleep. Nor is it selfishness that causes the "wise" bridesmaids to refuse to share with their less foresighted sisters. If they all share, they will all quickly run out of oil, plunging the feast into darkness. And it is precisely their task to illuminate the feast.

So the foolish ones go off to procure oil, and while they are gone the groom and his retinue arrive. When the "foolish" young girls finally return, they discover the feast has begun. The door is bolted and they can't get inside. They knock, but the groom refuses to allow them entry at the risk of allowing demons to enter and spoil the marriage.

When is the door closed to us, so that we can't join the feast? "Oil" in this story is in short supply. In our day it will soon be so for the entire world's oil supply, and then we will begin talking about conservation, after the door is already shut. We simply assume we can burn our lights the way we do and have light indefinitely.

Six million children die of malnutrition and hunger-related causes every year. That's 16,400 every day.[1] Most of that is preventable. Bread for the World believes that hunger can be wiped out for only a few billion dollars—peanuts compared with the military budgets of the world powers. If we don't respond, these children will find the door barred in their faces—and in their case, they weren't "foolish" but innocent. *We* will be the fools, but it will be too late for those who already face that closed door.

Jesus is not warning about the last judgment here, but against a judgment already taking place every day. In the world's midnight, Jesus brought the reign of God to humanity. Jesus transformed the world's midnight from a time of destitution into a time of celebration. Will we be at the wedding feast or locked out by our failure to grasp

---

1. U.N. Food and Agriculture Organization, *State of Food Insecurity in the World,* 2002.

the meaning of that closed door? Perhaps there will be later feasts I can say yes to and be prepared for, but I have for all time missed the chance for this feast. The times we haven't responded to God's invitations to act add up to our unlived life. It is difficult to die with so much lost opportunity.

Children's Time [LH]

It's entirely possible that the children have never seen a lamp lit with oil, or at least did not recognize that's what it was or how it works. Many of us nowadays have decorative oil lamps, and while they aren't like what the bridesmaids in the story would have carried, think about bringing one, already lit, into the sanctuary. Talk about how the oil and wick work, and how the oil gets used up as the lamp burns. Given the age of your children, you may not be able to make the point Walter Wink does about non-renewable resources, such as oil, being used up. Instead, you may be able to talk about the importance of light in our lives, light that takes away the darkness and calms our fears, and the light of life that Jesus brings. We can take none of these for granted, but we can give thanks for each.

Musical Suggestions [LH]

We Will Serve the Lord (Haas)—GC 869

We Will Serve the Lord (Cooney)—GC 665

Let There Be Light—UMH 440

Keep Your Lamps Trimmed and Burning—NCH 369

Christ's Word to Us Is Like a Burning Fire—BP 155

Walter Wink

Thirty-Third Sunday in Ordinary Time

RCL: Judges 4:1-7; Psalm 123; 1 Thessalonians 5:1-11; Matthew
25:14-30

LM: Proverbs 31:10-13, 19-20, 30-31; Psalm 128:1-2, 3, 4-5;
1 Thessalonians 5:1-6; Matthew 25:14-30 or 25:14-15, 19-21

In modern times the parable of the Talents has been understood to
mean earning power. Matthew may have understood it as natural abilities (v. 15); others, as divine gifts. How might Jesus have intended it?

These readings all assume that God is the master and we are the servants. But then a wonderful thing happened in a maximum security
prison in New York State, where biblical scholar Robert T. Fortna had
taken a class of undergraduates. The parable of the Talents was the
subject of the study that night. What follows is a condensed recon-
struction of that conversation:

FORTNA: Our agenda is the parable of the Talents. I suggest we try to
discover what Jesus' original story was and what it means.

JOEY: Well, we all know that. It's about our talents God gave us, how
we should use them.

FORTNA: Are you sure?

SEVERAL INMATES: Of course. Hell yes. What else could it mean?

FORTNA: But why does Jesus tell this long and complicated story just
to say that?

INMATES: You tell us, Prof; that's your thing. *[Laughter, not derisive.]*

FORTNA: Well, I'm not sure I know. *[Murmuring.]*

RED: Joey told you what it means. Ain't he right?

FORTNA: I don't think so.

INMATES: Then why does it talk about talents?

A STUDENT *[to the teacher's relief]*: It can't be about talents, because in the story that word means a lot of money and doesn't have anything to do with what we call talent.

RED: Well, look at the story. It says, "Each according to his ability." Don't that mean talent?

STUDENT *[taken aback]*: Well, maybe . . .

JOEY: What does she mean, "maybe"? Whatcha teaching these kids, Prof?

FORTNA: I try to get them to look at the text . . . and Red got us started.

JOEY: Yeah, like I said, the story means we should use our talents what God gave us; some does better at that than some others. *[Looking around with a grin.]*

SMITTY: Hey, Joey; what use you got for talents? You in here for life, man. *[Laughter, easy and affectionate from the inmates, nervous from the visitors.]*

FORTNA *[trying hard]*: We tend to assume that the rich man who went away stands for God. Can we be sure of that?

INMATES: It's obvious. All these stories are about God.

FORTNA: Look, let's study the story just the way it's told. What do you think of the three slaves?

SMITTY: Two of them is smart, one kinda slow.

FORTNA: So if you were the man who buried the money, you'd punish him too?

RED: Of course the rich dude gonna punish him; he was this "unprofitable servant."

SMITTY: Yeah, my Bible say he was worthless.

FORTNA: Do you agree?

ALL: Why not?

JOEY: Prof, this is gettin' us nowhere. We all understand this story; let's talk 'bout somethin' useful.

FORTNA *[a little desperately, grasping at a straw]:* Wait a minute, Joey. Which of those three guys in the story do you like the best?

SMITTY *[after a pause, and with a little smile]:* Why, Prof, I like that third guy.

FORTNA: Okay, go with that. How do you feel about this boss who gave you all this money to invest for him?

SMITTY *[pausing]:* Why that son of a bitch! He tryin' to use me to make his money for him. And I get the rap in the end if I lose it.

FORTNA: So is he God?

JOEY: Of course not. Who said that anyway? *[Laughter.]*

Joey, with many of his fellow inmates, is one of the kind of people Jesus mostly addressed in his teaching—disenfranchised, rejected, oppressed. So perhaps his intuition, once the religious habits of his biblicist upbringing fell away, gives us a clue to this parable's meaning.

At roughly the same time that Fortna's class discovered new insight in this parable, Richard Rohrbaugh, Bruce Malina, Dom Crosson, and, shortly thereafter, William Herzog, were developing a similar rereading of this parable. What Smitty intuited from his social location these scholars have now independently demonstrated exegetically. The master is a rapacious aristocrat who really is the kind of man the third slave says he is. The servants know they must make a 100 percent profit; everything after that they can keep. They are the ones, then, who do the master's dirty work, exploiting others for profit, largely through loans with exorbitant interest. The master is happy to let them skim "honest graft" as he rewards their behaving like him.

But the third servant tells the master what all the poor wished they might: the master is a parasite, living off the labor of others without return to the peasants. By burying the money, he takes it out of circulation, where it can no longer be used to dispossess more peasants from their lands by usurious loans.

This parable, then, far from encouraging "developing our talents," is an indictment of the Powers That Be for reaping where they do not sow and gathering where they do not scatter seed. What do we, as advocates for people who are hungry, make of this story? If we can let go of identifying the master in the parable with God, we can read this as an indictment of a system that creates poverty and hunger. To endanger its profits, huge as they are, is to challenge the way money and goods are distributed.

Children's Time [LH]

The complexity of the Gospel story makes it challenging to suggest a clear approach. If you (or your pastor) plan to take a fairly conventional interpretation of "talent," you may be able to fashion some learning from that about causing the things we're entrusted with to grow and prosper.

An alternative is in the passage from 1 Thessalonians, which talks about the breastplate of faith and love and the helmet of the hope of salvation. Make sure you read the other Epistle passages (Romans 13:12; Ephesians 6:13-17) in which the armor metaphors appear. Children have probably seen books and movies about knights and will remember the protective gear they wear. What does that have to do with our loving God? How do we think about the care and protection that our faith in God offers? How is armor a good and also a troublesome way to think about God and faith?

Musical Suggestions [LH]

All Who Love and Serve Your City—UMH 433

Abundant Life—GC 710

We Are Called—FWS 2172

Let Justice Roll Like a River—GC 716

The Harvest of Justice—GC 711

Voices That Challenge—GC 721

Walter Wink

Christ the King

RCL: Ezekiel 34:11-16, 20-24; Psalm 100; Ephesians 1:15-23; Matthew
    25:31-46

LM: Ezekiel 34:11-12, 15-17; Psalm 23:1-2, 2-3, 5-6; 1 Corinthians
    15:20-26, 28; Matthew 25:31-46

Matthew 25:32 has been thoroughly contaminated by the doctrine
of the second coming of Christ. He comes in glory, his titles are King
and Lord, he sits on a glorious throne (any kitchen stool would have
done), he judges all the nations, and people are divided into "good"
and "bad" rather than being regarded as a mix of both. This parable,
which is the very heart and soul of social justice struggles in the
churches, treats the goats unjustly, since they were already goats before
the judgment began. There should have been good and bad goats, not
rejection by category. Conventional "sheep" who obey their leaders
and flock together are preferred here to gutsy goats, who go their own
way and eat virtually anything.

None of that touches the positive heart of the parable, however.
The "sheep" are surprised they are the elect; they were compassionate,
not in order to earn a reward, but simply because they were in solidarity with the sufferers. They just cared. Note that the judgment is not
between believers and unbelievers, or Christians and non-Christians,
or church members and non-church members. The judgment is not
even based on confessing Jesus as Lord and Savior or on being reborn.
It is wholly contingent on whether one has responded humanely and

compassionately to the needs of those who are marginalized, nameless, in prison, homeless, and disreputable. So great is the solidarity of humanity that when we do such acts of compassion to the very least, we do it for all humanity.

But that compassion begins to alter the parable itself, for when those who showed compassion see the tortures of the damned (which Matthew has liberally added in verses 41-46), will they not renounce heaven in order to minister to those writhing in eternal fire? For if the Human Being ("the son of the man") is in the "least of these" (*not* church members, as Matthew has it, but really down-and-out people), then is he not also in the "goats"? How can bad people be sent to hell if the Human Being is in them? If any are lost, are not all lost in them, and the Human Being as well? And how can all this be squared with Jesus' own words: "For the son of the man came to seek out and to save *the lost*" (Luke 19:10; author's translation)?

Besides, the compassionate people in the parable *did not know* that they were serving Sophia's Child, the Human Being, in their needy neighbors. But we, having read the parable, *do* know that the Human Being is in these poor, and so we have contrived to stand the parable on its head and make it the manifesto for social action as a form of works righteousness. How much clergy burnout takes its rise in this remarkable but double-edged parable? As one workshop participant said of this passage, "But I tried that for seven years and ignored my wife and family trying to get European and U.S. money to the starving of India and Africa. I totally ignored the 'least' within myself and my family, till I lost them through divorce. Only then did I wake up to the ignored 'least' within me. It's both outer and inner: we have to respond to the 'least' on both fronts."

Another surprise of the parable is in verse 32: "All the nations (*ta ethnē*, neuter) will be gathered before him, and he will separate people (*autous*, masculine) one from another. . . ." A pronoun must agree with its antecedent in gender and number. This one does not. This means that it is not the nations as such that are judged, but the individual members *(autous)* of the nations, and they will be judged by how their *nations* have treated the needy: what, in effect, were their systems of welfare, judiciary, prisons, and healthcare? The ultimate principle of humanness ("the son of the man") is here depicted as judging all people on the basis of how their nations have treated the marginalized of society. Each of us must take individual responsibility, insofar as we are able, for the behavior of the corporate systems to which we belong. What better reason do we need to speak out to our nation's leaders in solidarity with hungry people, as Bread for the World members do?

Children's Time [LH]

Today's Gospel urges us to see Christ's face in those who are on the margins and to respond with compassion and a commitment to justice. As we prepare over the next month for a season of giving, this message is ever more urgent. In a simple way with our children, we can ask them to do those kinds of things for each other and for those who are hungry and needy in your community, our nation, and the world. It may also be important to remind them that Christ is present in each of them. Affirm each child, if the number makes it possible, by saying something like, "I see Christ in you, Eric, because you are gentle and caring." "I see Christ in you, Shaunda, because you have energy and commitment." "I see Christ in you, Carlos, because you take time to pray."

Musical Suggestions [LH]

God of Day and God of Darkness—GC 761

Eternal Christ, You Rule—NCH 302

Bread for the World—GC 827

Whatsoever You Do—GC 670

There's a Spirit in the Air—PH 433

Barbara Lundblad

Watch Night/New Year

RCL: Ecclesiastes 3:1-13; Psalm 8; Revelation 21:1-6a; Matthew 25:31-46

New Year's Eve is a strange time. There are the same number of minutes and seconds as on every other night of the year, but we seldom count down the final ten seconds on other nights. Time itself takes on a different meaning as these precious last seconds pass, reminding us of time never to be retrieved again. We can't hold on to it any more than we can stop the last grains of sand from slipping to the bottom of the hourglass. This last night of the year brings a kind of wistfulness—regrets for wasted time and forgotten resolutions.

Yet there is also the promise of a new year filled with possibilities, a year untarnished by mistakes or broken dreams. Tonight's readings gather up both the regrets and the possibilities. "To everything there is a season," writes the Preacher, "and a time for every matter under heaven. A time to be born and a time to die; a time to plant and a time to pluck up what is planted" (Eccl 3:1-2). Tonight the rhythm of ending and beginning is etched against the night sky as the ball drops in Times Square: "Ten, nine, eight . . . Happy New Year!" And we add our own verse to the rhymes of Ecclesiastes: "A time to regret what has passed us by, and a time to hope for what lies ahead."

What will the days ahead bring? Some will dare to make resolutions both small and great, perhaps the same resolutions made a year ago! The readings from Revelation and Matthew both bring visions of the future: a new heaven and a new earth, the coming in glory of the Son of Man. What shall we do with these visions? "See, I am making all things new," says the one seated on the throne (Rev 21:5). One response is to wait for God to do everything: to bring justice, to wipe away tears, to put an end to crying and pain. Sometimes visions can lead to apathy. Yet this same vision declares, "See, the home of God is among mortals" (v. 3). God is at home with us as we count down the minutes and the seconds, as we imagine the days of the new year spread out shining and spotless before us.

What would it mean to believe that God is not far off but at home with us in the year ahead? God at the table with us at suppertime, God with us as we go to work, God at home with mortals (and there's no mention of God being at home with only one nation). Jesus brings that vision of God-with-us down to earth in life-changing ways. When he talks about the days to come, he says far less about heaven and hell than we imagine. Jesus doesn't ask the question, "If you die tonight, do you know where you will be?" (No doubt someone will be passing out tracts with that question tonight in Times Square.) Jesus' vision of the coming of the Son of Man spills over from the future into the present. The ones called "blessed" aren't described for their strong faith or their doctrinal assurance. We have no evidence that they have confessed their sins or accepted Jesus as their Lord and Savior. But they live as though God has made a home among them, creating brothers and sisters where strangers had been. What does such living look like? "I was hungry and you gave me food . . ." (Matt 25:35-36).

On this last night of the year we might hear Jesus calling us to save the leftovers from tonight's party for the soup kitchen down the street. We might resolve to take our old coats and sweaters to the homeless shelter before week's end. Those aren't bad ideas. But Jesus' vision is much bigger, more global: all nations will be gathered before the throne when the Son of Man comes in glory. All nations: the homeless on our streets and the children of Iraq, the sick friend in the hospital and the millions dying of AIDS in Africa, the hungry families coming to the food pantry in your church and the refugees lined up for cups of rice in camps across the world. Instead of making New Year's resolutions, write letters to congressional leaders and the President urging support for the most urgent Bread for the World campaign. Prepare sample letters beforehand. Take time during the service to write. Invite people to a New Year's procession to the mailbox after worship!

Children's Time

If children are included in this service, you might involve them in preparing and voicing a litany using as a refrain one of the verses from tonight's readings. "When did we see you, Lord?" or "See, the home of God is among mortals." Name specific countries and communities where people are hungry, threatened by war, driven from their homes. Name also signs of hope: wells dug to provide clean water, land mines removed to free farmland for crops, more U.S. aid allocated to provide food for people in Zimbabwe.

Musical Suggestions [LH]

I Come with Joy—UMH 617

Like A Mother Who Has Borne Us—NCH 583

When the Poor Ones (Cuando el Pobre)—BP 154

Now Greet the Swiftly Changing Year—NCH 431

By Gracious Powers—UMH 517

Barbara Lundblad

All Saints' Day

RCL: Revelation 7:9-17; Psalm 34:1-10, 22; 1 John 3:1-3; Matthew 5:1-12

LM: Revelation 7:2-4, 9-14; Psalm 24:1-2, 3-4, 5-6; 1 John 3:1-3; Matthew 5:1-12a

On this day our minds are filled with memories of loved ones who have died, not only in the year past but long ago. We close our eyes and see them still, and try to remember the sound of their voices. We wait for their names to be read aloud in worship, feeling the weight of loved ones' names in a particular way. When the passage from Matthew's Gospel is read aloud, one blessing seems to stand out among the rest: "Blessed are those who mourn, for they will be comforted" (v. 4). On this day the church sanctuary is filled with a great cloud of witnesses. "How many were in church today?" someone might ask you later. "Thousands!" you could reply, and you'd be right no matter how many the ushers counted.

The communion of saints gathers up the living and the dead in one eternal, sacred tapestry. This communion also extends into the future in the visions of Revelation: "After this I looked, and there was a great multitude that no one could count, from every nation, from all tribes and peoples and languages, standing before the throne and before the Lamb, robed in white" (v. 9). In these words we glimpse another dimension of the communion of saints. This communion transcends not only time but also space, taking us beyond our neighborhoods and national boundaries. Those gathered in the sanctuary are part of a global communion of saints too large to fit inside one church, people of every race and tongue and nation.

How can we hear today's readings with this global communion of saints in view alongside the blessed saints who live close within our memories? It isn't easy, for our emotions well up, and it's hard to hear anything other than the names we remember. The Gospel reading from Matthew can also be a problem, for the Beatitudes are so familiar that it's hard to hear them anew. Some have pointed out the differences between Matthew's blessings and those found in Luke, insisting that Luke is much more earthy. Where Matthew says, "Blessed are the poor in spirit," Luke says, "Blessed are you who are poor." Luke says, "Blessed are you who are hungry now," while Matthew says, "Blessed are those who hunger and thirst for righteousness." Does this mean that Matthew's Jesus is more "spiritual," not concerned about people who are actually poor and hungry? Some people make that assumption, turning the Beatitudes into lovely verses for needlepoint pillows, stripped of any connection to the earthly realities of poverty and hunger.

It is *righteousness* that stands at the center of Matthew's Beatitudes, named both in the middle (v. 6) and near the end (v. 10). What does it mean to hunger and thirst after righteousness? What does it mean to be persecuted for righteousness' sake? This word *righteousness* is very important for Matthew, and he doesn't leave us guessing what righteousness looks like. Righteousness looks like Joseph taking Mary for his wife—even though he had every reason to abandon her quietly (Matt 1:18-25). Righteousness looks like forgiveness rather than revenge, loving your enemies and praying for those who persecute you (Matt 5:38-48)—even though the written law called for "an eye for an eye and a tooth for a tooth." Righteousness looks like food shared with hungry people, a cup of water for the thirsty one, and clothing for those who are naked—even though it isn't obvious that the person in need is Jesus (Matt 25:31-46). Righteousness, often described as a passive gift, is very active in Matthew's Gospel. People *do* righteousness. They care for one another as family, forgive rather than avenge enemies, and make sure hungry people are fed.

We dare not confine the Beatitudes to a pillow covering or a bookmark. Jesus calls us to radical righteousness that connects us to the global communion of saints. In the prayers today we not only name the names of loved ones who have died but lift up the names, known and unknown, of men, women, and children who are hungry. It would be fitting on this All Saints' Day to bring not only our prayers but an offering of letters to government leaders, letters advocating justice for those who are in need. Even as we remember those closest to us who have died, we also remember Jesus' words to the righteous before the throne of glory: "Truly I tell you, just as you did it to one of the least of these who are members of my family, you did it to me" (Matt 25:40).

Children's Time

Find one of those expanding geometric balls (available at science museums or perhaps in some child's playroom). Close the ball up as small as it will go. Ask: "Who's part of God's family?" Children may name themselves, their parents, or people sitting in the pews. "What about people who are sick today?" Hopefully, children will say, "Oh, they're part of the church too." Expand the ball a bit larger. "What about people who have died?" Children might name a grandparent or someone close to them. Keep expanding the ball with each question. "What about people in other parts of the world (you might ask them to name countries they know), are they part of God's family?" Open the ball all the way. If you have a ball that's large enough, children can reach their hands inside and hold hands with someone "across the globe." With hands joined, pray for people around the world, especially for those in need. You might also give each child a postcard, pre-addressed to a senator or representative: "Please help hungry people in _____. Vote for (name a specific bill supported by Bread for the World)."

Musical Suggestions [LH]

All Who Hunger—FWS 2126

Blest Are They—GC 659

In Unity We Lift Our Song—FWS 2221

Barbara Lundblad

Thanksgiving Day

RCL: Deuteronomy 8:7-18; Psalm 65; 2 Corinthians 9:6-15; Luke 17:11-19

LM: Deuteronomy 8:7-18 or Sirach 50:22-24 or 1 Kings 8:55-61; Psalm 113:1-8 or Psalm 138:1-5; 1 Corinthians 1:3-9 or Colossians 3:12-17 or 1 Timothy 6:6-11, 17-19; Luke 17:11-19 or Mark 5:18-20 or Luke 12:15-21

Thanksgiving is the quintessential "American" holiday. (The word "American" here really means the United States, not Canada to the north nor the Americas to the south.) The fourth Thursday in November is our own peculiar national celebration, recalling the legend of food shared with starving pilgrims by Native American people, though seldom acknowledging the lands we took from them as our end of the bargain. This day is marked by rituals that celebrate "American" values: Macy's Thanksgiving Day Parade (shopping), football games (competition), and eating to excess (overconsumption of the world's goods). How can we faithfully worship God on a day when the rituals of the marketplace worship something else?

The reading from Deuteronomy can be especially helpful. It may seem like our founding fathers borrowed these words about the promised land: a land with flowing streams, wheat, and barley, a land where we can eat bread without scarcity. This country has been portrayed as a city set on a hill, a beacon to the rest of the world, from the earliest presidential addresses up to the present time. When politicians end their speeches saying, "God, bless America," we have a sense that this is a prayer for us alone and no one else. But we can't stop the reading with the glorious bounty of the promised land. The Deuteronomy text goes on: "Take care that you do not forget the Lord your God, by failing to keep his commandments" (v. 11). When you have entered this good land, when you have built houses, when your herds and flocks have multiplied and you have mined silver and gold, "Do not say to yourself, 'My power and the might of my own hand have gotten me this wealth'" (v. 17).

But we have said this. We have exalted ourselves and forgotten God. In her book *Chaos or Community,* Holly Sklar says, "The United States is the poorest rich country in the world," lagging behind other industrialized democracies in assuring basic human needs such as healthcare. Even more starkly, she writes, "If the U.S. government were a parent, it would be guilty of child abuse. . . . Mortality rates for black babies in the U. S. are intolerable; our country ranks way down the list behind such nations as Jamaica, Sri Lanka, Poland, Cuba, and Kuwait." Sklar summarizes the statistics saying, "We have a greed surplus and a justice deficit."[1]

We don't need to look far to see the human face of stark statistics. Lines at soup kitchens and food pantries have grown longer and longer since the welfare reform act was passed in 1996. According to America's Second Harvest, 39 percent of U.S. families receiving emergency food have at least one adult working. Of those seeking food assistance in 2000, more than eight million were children; no doubt that number is now even higher. Yet, during this same time, the number of millionaires in the U.S. doubled in just five years.[2] Tax cuts for the wealthiest citizens will ensure that this number rises even in an economic downturn, while the lines swell outside the food pantry doors. Current political leaders have called on the religious community to pick up the slack, to provide the safety net. Is this reasonable? In the year 2000, Rev. Fred Kammer of Catholic Charities provided a reality check: "If the religious community alone were expected to make up for the proposed cuts in government social spending . . . the task of replacement would require an average annual increase of $225,000 for charitable

---

1. Holly Sklar, *Chaos or Community: Seeking Solutions, Not Scapegoats, for Bad Economics* (Boston: South End Press, 1995) 11–13.
2. Leslie L. Norton, "The Wealth Revolution," *Barrons* (Sept. 18, 2000) 33.

works from each of the nation's 258,000 churches, synagogues and mosques. As a point of comparison, the *average total budget* of a congregation is only $100,000 per year."[3]

What promises are we keeping in this "promised land"? On this day dedicated to shopping, football, and extravagant eating, we're drawn back to the words of Deuteronomy, words about a bountiful land and about keeping promises to a bountiful God. This may be the day people serve Thanksgiving dinner at a shelter for homeless people, and the offering may include canned goods for the local food shelf. But we must also demand that our government do more to support the common good. Today is a very good time to receive an offering of letters: "Dear Senator, please use my tax money to support the common good. Give your support to (Bill No. _____). We have enough millionaires."

On this most "American" holiday, we might also sing an additional verse of "America the Beautiful":

> O beautiful, the world so wide,
> Our wondrous global home!
> God, shed your grace on ev'ry place,
> And not on us alone.
> America! America!
> God, help us now to see
> That ev'ry land is in your hand
> From sea to shining sea!

Children's Time [LH]

Take time to reflect with the children on the words that conclude Barbara Lundblad's reflection, her own additional verse to "America the Beautiful." How is our nation at its best when it understands that God's blessings and care extend to other places and people as well? How is Thanksgiving, a holiday based on traditions very rooted in our nation's history, also a symbol of what so many people in our world lack on a daily basis—adequate food. Pray that we all work for justice for hungry people on this day when food is so prominent in our midst.

3. Cited in The Employment Project newsletter, *No More Jobs,* vol. 6, no. 2 (Feb. 2000).

Musical Suggestions [LH]

Praise and Thanksgiving—GC 764

The Harvest of Justice—GC 711

Lord of All Nations, Grant Me Grace—BP 178

Take My Gifts—NCH 562

An Outcast among Outcasts—FWS 2104

Contributors

DAVID BECKMANN has been president of Bread for the World since 1991. He is both a Lutheran pastor and an economist and formerly served in several positions at the World Bank. Former Bread for the World communications staff member Aimee Moiso, now a seminarian at San Francisco Theological Seminary, helped him develop his reflections for this book.

GLEN BENGSON is pastor of First Evangelical Lutheran Church in Xenia, Ohio. Glen has been a member of Bread for the World since its founding in 1974 and served as Ohio state coordinator in the late 1990s. He has served in the U.S. Navy, taught math to seventh graders, serves on his ELCA denomination's Hunger Program, traveled to Puerto Rico, Haiti, Mexico, and the Middle East on various education trips, and coordinates the local CROP Walk.

AMY BOOKER-HIRSCH, an ordained pastor in the Christian Church (Disciples of Christ), first learned about Bread for the World as a college student at Arizona State University. She has helped feed children at a Disciples of Christ mission station in Zaire, worked with Central American refugees in Tucson, and is a hospital chaplain. She graduated from Northwest Christian College in Eugene, Oregon, with an M.A. and Phillips Theological Seminary in Enid, Oklahoma, with an M.Div.

WILLIAM J. BYRON, S.J., recently retired pastor of Holy Trinity Catholic Church in Washington, D.C., is research professor in the Sellinger School of Business at Loyola College in Maryland. He was a founding director and longtime chair of the board of Bread for the World. An economist by training, he is past president of the University of Scranton and The Catholic University of America. His biweekly column, "Looking Around," is syndicated through Catholic News Service.

JAMES M. DUNN is professor of Christianity and public policy at Wake Forest University Divinity School, Winston-Salem, North Carolina, and president of the Baptist Joint Committee Endowment, where he was executive director from 1980 to 1999. He was president of Bread for the World's Board in 1985–1986 and has been an activist for hunger concerns since 1966. He holds a Ph.D. in Christian social ethics from Southwestern Baptist Theological Seminary and honorary doctorates from six colleges and universities.

KAREN FITZPATRICK recently served on the Bread for the World board of directors and has been a BFW congressional district coordinator since 1980. She lives in Minnesota, where she enjoys organic gardening. Karen recently retired from her position as an adult educator at the Church of the Risen Savior, a large suburban Roman Catholic parish in Burnsville. She has been involved in social justice advocacy for most of her life around issues such as housing and globalization in addition to hunger.

LARRY HOLLAR is senior regional organizer with Bread for the World and formerly served as BFW's issues director. Trained in languages at Williams College, the law at Yale Law School, and biblical interpretation and theology at Wesley Theological Seminary, he served on the legal staff of a congressional committee and a federal executive department before joining the BFW staff in 1985. He is an ordained elder in the Presbyterian Church (U.S.A.), a professional biblical storyteller and singer, and is editor of this volume.

REVEREND AL KRASS has been a BFW member since the late 1970s, when he was a co-editor of "The Other Side." A former missionary of the United Church of Christ in Ghana, he has been associated with efforts for justice and peace and ecumenism wherever he has been. Retired and living in Levittown, Pennsylvania, he chairs the Metropolitan Christian Council of Philadelphia's Peacemaking Committee.

BARBARA LUNDBLAD served as pastor of Our Saviour's Atonement Lutheran Church in upper Manhattan for 16 years before joining the faculty of Union Theological Seminary in 1997. She is a longtime member of Bread for the World. The congregation she served was one of the founders of the Washington Heights Food Pantry and was involved in BFW letter-writing campaigns.

MARC MILLER, a pastor in the Evangelical Lutheran Church in America, received his Master's of Divinity through Christ Seminary-Seminex in St. Louis and Chicago. He has served parishes in Colorado, Utah, and Ohio, and is currently an Assistant to the Bishop of the Northwest Ohio Synod of the ELCA. In addition to serving as a Bread for the World district coordinator in Utah and Ohio, he also started a Habitat for Humanity chapter in Summit County, Utah.

THE REVEREND CANON SAUNDRA D. RICHARDSON is priest in charge at St. Matthew's and St. Joseph's Episcopal Church in Detroit, Michigan. Prior to that and when writing these reflections, she was assistant to the bishop for community witness, ecumenical/interfaith officer, and diocesan refugee coordinator for the Episcopal diocese of Michigan. Her work included networking and partnering the diocese with other denominations and faith groups, community and government entities with advocacy, witness, and justice issues for those least embraced by society. She is a member of Bread for the World and promotes the movement in the parish.

FELIPE SALINAS is director of college access and support programs at the University of Texas-Pan American, overseeing projects that prepare potential first-generation college students from low-income and migrant farm-worker families for post-secondary education. He holds a master of religious education from the University of Dallas and a master of arts in communication from UT-Pan American. Felipe also has 18 years experience as a Roman Catholic youth ministry coordinator at the parish and diocesan levels, has facilitated training in multicultural youth ministry for the Center for Youth Ministry Development, and serves on his parish Peace and Justice Commission in McAllen, Texas. He has been a longtime member of Bread for the World and has served on its board of directors.

REVEREND DONALD DIXON WILLIAMS is an ordained Pentecostal minister of the United Way of the Cross Church of Christ. A native of Washington, D.C., he has worked on the staff of Bread for the World for 16 years with a focus on racial/ethnic church relations.

He also serves as southeast consultant for the Institute for Recovery from Racisms in Detroit, Michigan.

DR. WALTER WINK is professor of biblical interpretation at Auburn Theological Seminary in New York City and previously taught at Union Theological Seminary and Hartford Seminary. His published works include a trilogy on the Powers and books on the transformational quality of the Bible. A well-known workshop leader on nonviolence and other themes throughout the world, Walter served as a United Methodist pastor in southeast Texas for five years and now attends Quaker meetings. He is a longtime member of Bread for the World.

Bread for the World

BREAD FOR THE WORLD is a 50,000-member Christian citizens' movement against hunger. Founded in 1974, Bread for the World's members lobby Congress and the Administration to bring about public policy changes that address the root causes of hunger and poverty in the United States and overseas. Bread for the World is a nonpartisan organization supported by 45 denominations and many theological perspectives. For more information, call 1-800-82-BREAD or see the movement's website, www.bread.org.

Scripture Index

The following index includes references to the readings of both the Revised Common Lectionary and the Lectionary for Mass, listing the more inclusive passage where readings differ. Page citations, given after the slash (/) mark, refer to the first page of the reflection for the day the passage appears. Writers sometimes do not address each passage assigned for that day, so the reader may not find a comment on that passage in the day's reflection.